Jim Britt's Cracking the Rich Code⁴

Inspiring Stories, Insights and Strategies from Entrepreneurs Around the World

STAY IN TOUCH WITH JIM AND KEVIN

www.JimBritt.com

www.JimBrittCoaching.com

www.KevinHarringtom.tv

For daily strategies and insights from top entrepreneurs, join us at

THE RICH CODE CLUB

FREE members site.

www.TheRichCodeClub.com

Cracking the Rich Code[4]

Jim Britt

All Rights Reserved

Copyright 2020

Cracking the Rich Code, LLC

10556 Combie Road, Suite 6205

Auburn, CA 95602

The use of any part of this publication, whether reproduced, stored in any retrieval system, or transmitted in any forms or by any means, electronic or otherwise, without the prior written consent of the publisher, is an infringement of copyright law.

Jim Britt

Cracking the Rich Code[4]

SKU # 2370000819703

Co-authors from Around the World

Jim Britt

Kevin Harrington

Noah Amparano

Kendra Steel

Herbert Lang

Joy Ross

Kelly Voorhees

Stacy Oliveri

Marcus Anthony Ray

Mike Skrypnek

Christina Kumar

Merrilee Sweeney

Ted Malley and Kim Levings

Aimee Bucher

Lynette McDonald

Lauren Brenner

Christine Rose

Allen Hacker

Nadene Joy

Lilia Ackerman

Danielle Edmondson

DEDICATION

Entrepreneurs will change the world. They always have and they always will.

To the entrepreneurial spirit that lives within each of us.

God Bless America!

Foreword by Kevin Harrington

You probably know me as one of the "Sharks" on the hit TV show Shark Tank, where I was an investor in many entrepreneurial ventures.

But my life and business was not always like that. I used to be your regular, everyday

guy patching cracked driveways to make money. I had hopes and dreams just like most, yet I worked around people who didn't support my dreams. But you know what? I not only found a way out, but I found a way to my dreams... and so can you.

Now, I wake up every morning excited about my day, and I surround with only the people I want in my life; entrepreneurs who really want something more than just getting by paycheck to paycheck.

Today we hear stories -- mostly from the mainstream media -- everyday about how bad things are, businesses are closing and jobs being lost, interest rates are on the rise, how the gap between rich and poor is growing and how you'll never make it on your own.

But here's what I know for sure. Entrepreneurs are going to change the world. We always have and we always will.

Forget the 1% vs the 99%. 100% of us entrepreneurs need answers. We need solutions. We need something more than what we're being told by those who don't have a clue. We need to start saying Yes! to opportunity and No! to all the noise.

The fact is that it's a new world and a new economy. The "proven" methods of doing business and investing that produced successful results, even two years ago, simply may not work anymore.

If you want to succeed (or even survive) in our new world, you need an entirely new set of skills and information.

You need to "reposition" yourself...often.

You need to revamp how you do business...often.

You need to change how you handle and invest your money...often.

Like any other situation, if you know WHAT to do and WHEN to do it, you'll not only be "safe"... you could easily skyrocket financially.

If you have the right knowledge for today, the right opportunities for today, the right strategies for today and most of all the right character and mindset for today, you can win — and you can win big!

What I've discovered in my over three-decade career as an entrepreneur, is that success in the face of financial adversity boils down to 3 things:

The right knowledge at the right time.

The right opportunities at the right time.

The right you... ALL the time.

The bottom line is this: you can no longer afford to rely on anyone else to navigate your financial future. You have to rely on your "self." The question is... do you have a "self" you can rely on? Unfortunately, when it comes to entrepreneurship and money, many people don't. They don't have the financial education, the mental toughness, the knowledge and the skills to build wealth... especially in an ever-changing marketplace. You need to get RE-educated. You need to REINVENT yourself for success in the new economy. You need to learn new strategies in the areas of business and career, finance and real estate that create wealth or at least financial freedom in today's new world. But that's not all...

Skills and strategies and all that profound new knowledge won't do you one bit of good if you don't have the CHARACTER, the HABITS and the MENTALITY it takes to get rich. If you have internal barriers, your road to success will be slow and full of pain and struggle. It's like driving with one foot on the gas and one foot on the brake and always wondering why you aren't getting anywhere. Your mind is working against you instead of for you.

I have seen business owners come to me with their business ready to go under — and have the next year be their best financial year ever. I've see others that had a business that should skyrocket, yet fail because they didn't have the mental toughness to go the distance. I have seen people stuck in dead-end, dreary jobs break out of their rut, get involved in a brand-new passion, and become wildly successful.

No matter what you do for a living...regardless of your education, level of business experience or current financial status...If you have a burning desire for financial change then you won't want to miss this rare opportunity to learn from the entrepreneurs within this book.

It will provide you with some of the same success strategies that Jim Britt and I have used personally and shared with tens of thousands of people who've had tremendous financial success...people just like you, who wanted to get out of the rat race and enjoy financial freedom.

In addition, you'll learn what others have done, mistakes they made and how you can avoid them. You'll discover strategies that could make your business into a major market leader. I always say, "Just one good idea can change everything."

Success is predictable if you know what determines it. This book offers some valuable tips, knowledge, insights, skill sets, that will challenge you to leap beyond your current comfort level. If you want to strengthen your life, your business and your effectiveness overall, you'll discover a great friend in this book. You'll probably want to recommend it to all your entrepreneurial friends.

Although I haven't followed Jim Britt's career over the last 43 years, but I do know that he is recognized as one of the top thought leaders in the world, helping millions of people create prosperous lives. He has authored 13 books and multiple programs showing people how to understand their hidden abilities to do more, become more and enjoy more in every area of life. I also want to recognize Joel Sauceda, our online business partner. He is the brains behind the many online PR, Marketing, Branding and Lead Generation strategies each entrepreneur coauthor and reader of the book will benefit from.

The principles, concepts and ideas within this book are sometimes simple, but can be profound to a person who is ready for that perfect message at the right time and is willing to take action to change. Maybe for one it's a chapter on leadership or mindset. For the next, it's a chapter on raising capital, or securing a business loan. Each chapter is like opening a surprise empowering gift.

The conclusion to me is an exciting one. You, me and every other human being are shaping our brains and bodies by our attitude, the decisions we make, the intentions we hold and the actions we take daily. Why is it exciting? Because we are in control of all these things and we can change as long as we have the intention, willingness and commitment to look inside, take charge of our lives and make the changes.

I want to congratulate Jim Britt for making this publication series available and for allowing me to write the foreword, a chapter in each book and be involved with the entrepreneurs within this book and series. I honor Jim and the coauthors within this book and the series for the lives they are changing.

As you enter these pages, do so slowly and with an open mind. Savor the wisdom you discover here, and then with interest and curiosity discover what rings true for you, and then take action toward the life you want.

So many people settle for less in life, but I can tell you from my experience that it doesn't have to be that way.

Be prepared…because your life and business, is about to change!

Jim Britt & Kevin Harrington

As co-creators of this book series Jim Britt and Kevin Harrington have devoted their lives to helping others to live a more prosperous, fulfilled and happy life. Over the years they have influenced millions of lives through their coaching, mentoring, business strategies and leading by example. They are committed to never ending self-improvement and an inspiration to all they touch. They are both a true example that all things are possible. If you get a chance to work with Kevin and Jim or becoming a coauthor in a future Cracking the Rich Code book, jump at the chance!

Table of Contents

Foreword by Kevin Harrington vii

Jim Britt 1
    Reinvent Your Money Philosophy 2

Kevin Harrington 19
    Becoming A KPI 20

Noah Amparano 29
    It's Just a Choice 30

Kendra Steel 41
    Pandemic to Prosperous 42

Herbert Lang 53
    The Kindness Bridge to Wealth 54

Joy Ross 63
    The Pursuit of Excellence 64

Lauren Brenner 73
    Fuel Your Fire and Own It 74

Kelly O'Keefe Voorhees 83
    Be Fearless in Faith in Your Body, Heart and Soul 84

Jim Cocks 95
    An Entrepreneur's Biggest Challenge – Get Out of Your Own Way 96

Kim Levings & Ted Malley 105
    If you could think your way to success, why isn't everyone a success? 107

Princess Merrilee of Solana 119
    Why Love is Always the Answer 120

Nadene Joy 129
   Strategies to Help Business Professionals That are Stuck 130
Lynette McDonald 141
   Can Anyone Really Prosper from Behind B.A.R. s? 142
Christina Kumar 149
   In it to Win it 150
Lilia Ackerman 159
   Transforming Pain to Purpose 160
Christine Rose 169
   Sixteen Secrets to True Riches 170
Stacy Oliveri 179
   Zugzwang 180
Aimee Bucher 185
   What Happens When Companies Focus on Employee Happiness?
   186
Marcus Anthony Ray 193
   Cash in Your Failures for Success 194
Monica Griffin 201
   More to Life 202
Mike Skrypnek 209
   How do you give $1 million to charity every year? 210
A Allen Hacker 219
   Subliminal Self Sabotage: Causes and Corrections 220
Danielle Edmondson 229
   Angelosophy: Ambassador of Light 230
Afterword 239

Jim Britt's
Cracking the Rich Code⁴

Jim Britt

Jim Britt is an internationally recognized leader in the field of peak performance and personal empowerment training. He is author of 13 best-selling books, including *Rings of Truth; The Power of Letting Go; Freedom; Unleashing Your Authentic Power; Do This. Get Rich-For Entrepreneurs; The Flaw in The Law of Attraction;* and *The Law of Realization,* to name a few. He is the creator of a collaborative book series for entrepreneurs *Cracking the Rich Code.*

Jim has presented seminars throughout the world sharing his success principles and life-enhancing realizations with thousands of audiences, totaling over 1,500,000 people from all walks of life.

Jim has served as a success counselor to over 300 corporations worldwide. He was recently named as one of the world's top 20 success coaches, top 50 speakers and presented with the best of the best award out of the top 100 contributors of all time to the direct selling industry.

As an entrepreneur, Jim has launch 28 business ventures in the past 43 years and knows how to guide beginning and seasoned entrepreneurs toward a successful venture and avoid the classic mistakes made by the majority of new business launches.

Jim is more than aware of the challenges we all face in making adaptive changes for a sustainable future.

Reinvent Your Money Philosophy

By Jim Britt

Once again that uncomfortable feeling pays a visit, but this time you can't close the door and just ignore it. The discomfort that you are feeling is with yourself. You feel like your life does not fit you anymore. Maybe it hasn't for a long time. But do you dare reinvent yourself and your money philosophy? Do you have the courage to take the necessary steps to let go of the person you are today, and used to be, so that you can blossom into the person you have always wanted to become financially? This can sometimes feel scary because you have to let go of attachments you have about money in order to reinvent your new money philosophy. If you are up to the reinventing yourself and ready to travel along a new path to where you have never been, now is the perfect time to get started, and I want to help.

The process of reinventing yourself is very empowering. In fact, you can apply this philosophy to any area of your life. If you want something more in any area of life you have to reinvent yourself into someone different than you are today. But this is about reinventing your money philosophy.

You might not realize it yet, but you do have all it takes to truly ignite change financially.

Don't let anybody else tell you otherwise. The first thing you will need to do is take a look at yourself. What do you want to change about yourself? Because all change starts inside you.

Since you are starting over so to speak, if you are going to dream, might as well dream big. Think of yourself as an author who is writing your new life story, your new money philosophy. You are limited only by your imagination. Before you start reinventing yourself, you have to at least know what you're working with and what you want changed. The more specific you are, the better. This will give you direction and allow you to focus on the right things. If you ask someone what the most important thing in their life is, most often they will answer "family" or "their health." But is that actually true?

When you look at where the average person spends most of their waking hours, it is focused on making money. So, money must be the most important area for most…at least until they have all they want to feel financially secure. Again, since you are reinventing yourself and your money philosophy, if you are going to dream, you might as well dream big. So, what's the secret to incredible financial success? The secret is, there is no <u>one</u> secret! The reality is there are many "secrets" that work together in combination with one another, giving you the winning "combination" to succeed financially! Think of financial success like a giant vault at the bank with a thick steel door blocking it and a combination lock. Unless you have the right combination to that lock, it doesn't matter how much you beat on the door, how hard you work, how many lists you make, or good intentions you have. Because there is a combination you must know to unlock that door and get it to swing open so you can walk through to the other side where the money is.

Many years ago, I met a very wealthy person and I asked what inspired him to be wealthy? His answer really surprised me. He said, "Money is a game and the person with the most notches on his belt wins." I was shocked! I was a young man at the time and having grown up without much I wanted to become wealthy. Yet after hearing this person's response, I looked deeper into his eyes and frankly, he didn't seem all that happy, and the sense of lack of balance in his life was apparent. He was out of shape and had a look in his eyes of anxiety, loneliness and anger. I could tell that he had stepped on a lot of people to get to where he was. I knew right then I didn't want to take his approach.

How about you? Do you think that being financially wealthy takes putting yourself first and trampling over those that get in your way? Hopefully not. Do you think that being wealthy means putting the lust for money ahead of everything else? I sure hope not. On the other hand, I've met very wealthy people who give back to their community, have large circles of friends, and always seemed to be happy and abundant in so many other ways. In fact, a couple years ago I took a camera crew around the country and interviewed 11 self-made mega millionaires and one billionaire. The requirement was that they all had to have started with nothing. In other words, they didn't inherit their wealth. And all 12 made their money in different industries…

Internet marketing, network marketing, traditional business, real estate, television, direct sales, social media, etc. If you asked any of these twelve individuals the same question, you'd likely get this sort of answer: "Wealth is simply a vehicle that magnify your deeper personality traits and mindset."

The following is what I have learned from my own experiences and the experiences of these 12 mega-millionaires and others I have associated myself with over the years. Wealth is the ultimate power of leverage. It gives you options as to how you want to live. Nothing is truer about becoming wealthy than this. It is a magnifying glass into your money mindset and philosophy.

Wouldn't it be nice if you could simply decide to become wealthy and you did? Well, let me fill you in on a big secret…you can! You already know the basics. You know that you should pay off your debt and start budgeting. You know that all you need to do is regularly invest money into your savings and other investments and let time do the work. Spend less, save more, build your investment portfolio…you've heard it time and time again. Then why aren't you on the way to becoming wealthy? Maybe you are. If so, congratulations. There are many reasons that people don't take action, even though they have the information. The reality is that so many people are just simply afraid to change. Fear takes a lot away from a person. They don't want to fail but when you buy into fear it will take you down that path.

Here's one key to the vault's combination lock. For things to change for you financially, you have to make a change, otherwise you'll continue to keep producing the same results you've been producing. This may come as a shock to you, but most people really don't want to change.

Just give them a beer, point them toward the sofa and give them the television remote and a bag of chips. They will continue to complacently live out their lives, and complaining about what they don't have, and criticizing others for what they have. Their wealth philosophy is to earn a living and get by. They spend the majority of their time focused on what they *don't have* and what they *don't want*, on how to pay the bills, instead of focusing on what they *do have* and what they *do want* in their lives. Nothing wrong with this philosophy if that is what you want. But if it is not what you want, then *everything* is wrong with that philosophy.

I know people, as I'm sure you do, that love having the drama of being up to their ears in debt.

It's a balance beam that keeps excitement in their lives. It's a roller coaster ride that is thrilling, but always drops them off at the same place time and time again. But at such a huge cost! What they don't realize is that they can't maintain their balance or thrill forever. At some point you have to decide where to get off… or you simply fall off!

Most have been conditioned to believe that creating wealth is difficult, or that it's only for the lucky few. They convince themselves that "someday" they are going to be a success, to start their own business, to make a financial plan for their future, to have all they want in life…someday. Someday…what an interesting concept. Think of all the things that were supposed to have happened by now…that someday that you may have convinced yourself was just around the corner. To most, that someday is where they have convinced themselves they would be right now, if only they had more time, more talent, more education, more money, or maybe a better opportunity available. One of the things I discovered is that wealthy people think differently. They don't wait until someday. They decide and execute. They do things that the majority of people are not willing to do.

Before going any further, I would urge you to stop right now and take a realistic look at your last five years. Have you truly made progress? Are the last five years what *you* wanted? Are you where you thought you would be today financially? And, most importantly, do you have a solid plan for the next five? Too many people like to complain, but just don't want to make the effort. They don't have time. They'll do it next year. Let me tell you, you have to find time to get your financial situation in order if you want to gain wealth…and freedom…ever! Time is costing you money. The more time you spend trying to pay off credit cards, the more you pay the credit card company and contribute to their wealth. I'm not saying to ignore your financial obligations. What I'm saying is that paying off your credit cards, although a good place to start, will not bring you wealth. Why? Because after you pay them off you are still left with the mentality that charged them to the max in the first place. You *can* have all the money you want. It just takes learning and developing the traits that rich people use, and some time to make it happen. If you want to change your financial situation you have to reinvent yourself, because the old you won't cut it. To become wealthy, you will need to develop some vital traits.

Let me offer you the number sequence to the vault. First is a firm decision to become wealthy. Wealthy people you will find make solid decisions and commit to seeing them through. And decisions always come before the answers. Those who are *not* financially successful put off decisions or mess around with their decision once it is made... and have a lot of excuses why things are not working. That is the language of the poor. Mediocrity cannot be an option if you want to attain wealth. And wealth is whatever you say it is. A decision to be wealthy creates a wealth mindset, and your mindset determines how you show up in the world. I'm not talking about deciding *how* to make the money. Again, decision comes first, then the how to.

It is really surprising though, how many people fear making that decision. They do all sorts of things to keep the moment of decision at arms-length including:

Gathering more data.

Getting ready to get going...

As soon as this or that happens, I'll get going...

I need to do more research...

I need to get some other's opinion...

Fretting over who the decision might offend.

Worrying about the resources needed to pull off the decision.

Or hoping they will just get lucky and make the money they need without making a decision, etc.

The real problem is that most are stuck in a comfort zone and making a decision would possibly mean having to do something different, that might be a bit painful. I suppose that is a decision we all face…the pain of staying stuck in our current situation or the pain of change. Most people would rather live with the "old you" for fear that becoming the "new you" would be too painful.

If that is you, then you can close the book now, and get back to the TV and potato chips. If you are not willing to make a decision to change no one can help you.

Let's say you make a decision to be wealthy. Whatever wealth means to you. What happens next when the old programs, the old habit patterns and mind chatter kicks in? "Wait a minute! What makes you think you have the talent to become wealthy?" "I've never done it before! "Maybe I really can't become wealthy." "Besides, I don't have the expertise, time, money, etc., to become wealthy." And before long all the self-talk has changed your decision into something totally different from becoming wealthy. Wealth is a mindset.

I remember a friend of mine had created a hair care line that grew hair to go into drugstore chains. He had the connections to get it into the stores across the country. However, after months the line just wasn't selling. Instead of just giving up, a business associate told him about a new marketing concept, a TV infomercial. This was one of the first, if not the first, TV infomercial ever produced. So, nobody knew if it would actually work. My friend was a decision maker and a doer, so he said let's do it. That decision turned into over $200 million in sales that netted him almost $100 million. The point is, he could have given up with his first attempt. Again, wealth is a mindset.

One of the mega millionaires I interviewed went bankrupt three times and today has a net worth of over $500 million. My point is that you don't give up just because one approach to becoming wealthy doesn't work. There are thousands of ways to become wealthy, but without a wealth mindset nothing…ever… happens.

Remember this: <u>Every income level requires a different you</u>. You have to reinvent yourself, your mindset, your money philosophy, for each new income level. You have to be willing to let go of the *old you* and embrace the challenge of becoming the *new you*. And, if you want to learn, grow and change, you have to hang around people that challenge you to become better. If you want to become a million dollar a year earner, but yet you hang around and take input from people earning $60,000 a year, you'll likely to be right where they are financially. I'm not putting them down. I'm just saying that those you hang around most is what you become.

I know people, as I'm sure you do, who go to work every day to a job that they hate. They hate what they earn and/or what they do, but they stay because they feel they have no other choice. They justify their position by calling it job security. But what they don't realize is that there is no security in a job! Unless you are a smart investor, it's called *prolonged poverty* in my book! It's like living in a place you hate but you're afraid to move because of your job. Then you lose your job and can't afford to move, so you look for another insecure position that will keep you in the place you hate. *That's a sort of insanity, don't you think?*

What would I say to a person in that position? "If you want to get better, you have to make better decisions, and you have to hang out with and take input from those who've done what you want to do." I would say "if you want to be rich, you have to stop working for someone else's goals and dreams and make a decision to start working for your own." If you want to become wealthy, you have to stop with the employee mentality, reinvent yourself, and start thinking like wealthy people think."

The first step is to make the decision, one that doesn't allow for anything less. Up until the decision is made nothing happens...except, of course, the decision to stay where you are now. In reality not making a decision is a decision to leave everything status quo.

The next trait all wealthy people have in common is that they are bold. Financially successful people have learned that action is vital. And often times that requires a level of boldness. They know that procrastination kills. They live with the reality of consequences and know there will always be uncertainty in decisions, but they boldly step forward and make the decision anyway.

Just like my friend with the hair care product. No one can see all possible ramifications; no one can predict every contingency; no one can absolutely prevent failure…or assure success. However, the wealth minded person knows that failure is not final. It's just one of those possible outcomes that happens on their way to success. The real danger surrounding decision making is not "Will I make the wrong decision," but "Did I make the best decision possible given the facts and circumstances." Success minded individuals invest in learning what they need to make the correct decisions from those who have done what they want to do. But, when it comes to investing in mentorship, so often I hear people say "I can't afford it." "It costs too much." When in reality they can't afford not to." And without mentorship, it costs…way… too much!

I remember the time when my home was in foreclosure, both my vehicles and all my furniture had been repossessed …and I had less than a dollar to my name. Then, someone, a mentor, sat with me for two hours, helped me to get my head on straight, taught me a few things, and eliminated some mistakes… and my business took off like a rocket… to the tune of a million dollars in the next 12 months… back when a million was really a million. Wealthy people look at value not cost. What will the investment make them rather than what it will cost them?

The real question is, "What do you really want?" Are you just dreaming about success and wealth or standing on the sidelines observing other people's successes and wishing you had what they have? Do you justify why you are not financially successful? Or are you bold enough to take responsibility, step out into the spotlight and take center stage before you have all the answers?

Do you really want to be rich? And if so, what would financial success look like to you? Most people have never defined what financial success would be for them, and that's why they've never made a decision and taken bold action to have it. And that is the only reason they don't have it! The two most important question that you can ask yourself is, "Have I defined what financial success means to me?" And two, "Am I basing my future financial success on past experiences?" How you answer those questions can change your life!

Often times there is a feature in the investment section of some of the entrepreneurial magazines. It's a success story column on people who've made it big financially. You'll find stories of individuals who have carved out a niche for themselves in selected fields, lived a fulfilled life serving others with their skills and amassed quite a fortune while doing so. You will always find one common trait in all the featured personalities. Not in one of them. Not some of them. But this trait is in all of them! It is called a "wealth mindset." Despite the fact that they're from different backgrounds, all of them possess the same philosophy when it comes to money. Wealthy people think differently. This is the infamous "money consciousness" that most of the motivational and personal development trainers speak of so often in their books and seminars.

This wealth philosophy basically means this: Regardless of the physical condition that you may be currently in, as long as you see yourself bathing in financial abundance, your actions will maneuver and circumstances will unfold in a way to create the wealth that you see yourself enjoying. If you possess that wealth mindset, you will have the Midas touch when it comes to earning money. If you don't, you won't. That simple. The fortunate thing is all of us possess the innate ability to fire up this wealth mindset.

But the key is letting go of the old you and reinventing the new you that you want to become.

First is making the decision to be wealthy. Second is being bold. Next, is letting go of your limiting beliefs about money and changing how you relate to money. Some people frown at the mere mention of money. How many times have you heard people say something like this: "Oh, I'm not doing this for the money" or "Money isn't everything." Well, they're not wrong. Money isn't everything. The fact is that money in itself has no value. It is the things that money can buy when in circulation that makes it so valuable. Money can buy material possessions for sure. But personal freedom is what we all seek, and we all deserve to have what we want. Money gives you options. Those who say that money doesn't matter, I can guess with 100% accuracy that they are broke! How could you not be if "money doesn't matter" is their focus? At the same time, if you look from a different angle, once you've got enough money to be financially free, it can literally change what you do from laborious work to spending more precious moments with your family and friends as well as doing the things you love. In essence, if you never come to terms with what money can bring forth into your life, its real value, your uneasiness with the "idea" of money, it will limit your ability to create more of it.

To put it simply, just imagine this: would you go into a car showroom if you've never had the intention to purchase a car? You may not want to buy it now, but the fact that you walked into the showroom implies that you appreciate the value of what a car brings. It can serve as a means of transportation for you and your family. And because of the perceived value you see in owning a car, you'll find the means and ways to get one. Having money is the same. Once you see its value, believe you can have it, and want it like it is as essential as owning a car, you'll find the ways and means to getting it. Heck. Even those that are broke and spend their last few dollars on lottery tickets see the value of money. Remember, you can't create something that you're not in harmony with or that you haven't decided to have. Therefore, it becomes imperative that before you move onto other steps to really "get" this wealth mindset concept, you should definitely have a conversation with yourself, or someone that can mentor you, to let go of the beliefs, if you have them, that's limiting you about money.

Having money means…finish the sentence…

What came up? Do you feel your answer will move you toward being wealthy?

Answer these questions:

Why do you deserve to be wealthy?

What do you believe about money?

How did you come to believe this?

Who taught you to believe that way?

Were they wealthy?

Who taught them?

Is my money mindset based on past experiences or beliefs?

The only way to change a limiting belief is to challenge it. A belief is something that you have decided is true...it may not be at all. A belief is simply a decision that something is true...and it may have been made by someone else and passed down to you. The good news is that you can change a belief simply by changing your decisions and letting go of your old programming. If you want to be wealthy, you have to first decide to be wealthy...whatever being wealthy means to you.

The next combination to the vault is to decide "why" you want to be wealthy. What is the payoff for wealth? Why you want something is the fuel, the passion, that will take you where you want to go. It fuels the passion behind the decision. Everyone has the right to be wealthy. You have the right to be wealthy....and yet, most allow a temporary lack of money to eat into their minds, literally confining them into a vicious cycle of mediocrity. The bottom line is that people are not wealthy because they have not yet decided to be wealthy. So long as you make a conscious decision to become wealthy and have utmost faith that you can achieve it, and you let go of your outdated beliefs about money, you will act accordingly to what you believe. So, why not say "yes" to getting wealthy today! And say it with conviction. Deciding to be wealthy only gets you started on the quest, but what sustains you throughout the journey is the "why" you want to be wealthy, and letting go of the mind chatter that pulls you back into your old habit patterns.

What is the real reason that you want an extra $1 million in your bank account, or you want to earn a million dollars a year? Again, wealth is whatever you say it is. Could be $10,000 a month coming in from investments. What I know for sure is that, if you do not have a burning desire supporting your decision, and you don't let go of your old way of thinking and believing, you'll find your inspiration tapering off sooner and your decision fading into something totally different to being wealthy. That is the trap that most everyone falls into.

Try this exercise. Take a piece of paper and scribble down all the reasons that you can think of why you want to be wealthy. Maybe you would like to retire earlier and travel around the world? Or you want to quit your job and be a full time parent? Write down as many reasons as you can think of. Needless to say, the one that resonates with the deepest part of your heart should be written on an index card to remind you of the outcome you desire. Paste it to your forehead!

Again, wealth can be whatever you say it is. For some it might mean 10 million in the bank. For others it might mean having enough residual income coming monthly to completely cover their overhead. For example, if it's $5,000 per month that you're looking for, working in your existing job and going for a raise in pay might suffice. However, if $100,000 per month is what you intend to achieve, other alternatives such as starting your own business, investing in properties or working on your skills sets to better serve the marketplace will probably be more effective. More importantly, knowing how much you want prepares your mind for the potential issues you may face to make that happen. The more you want, the more challenges you face to get it. The challenge therefore becomes: how do you know how much you want? Arbitrarily quoting a figure will probably do you more harm than good. If the amount you pull out of the sky is much higher than what you really want, your approach to acquire the wealth may not be in harmony with why you want it and you may end up burning yourself out. In the event that the amount is lesser than what you really want, then you'll find yourself re-adjusting why you want it, which may not inspire you to keep going. Your "what" your "why" and your "decision" and "mindset" needs to be in harmony.

How you get there is not important at this moment. Suppose you want to get from point "A" to point "B." There's route 1, route 2, 3 all the way to infinity. When you believe that there is only one way to get there, it limits your possibilities. When you are totally open to how to get there, the mind starts considering the many options and may prompt you to act on one of them that you haven't even thought of before. Along the way, your wealthy mindset may allow you to recognize different opportunities, encouraging you to change course and go through a totally different experience than originally planned.

I remember steve who attained wealth in a totally different manner than expected. Initially, his plan was to market his own music compositions through conventional methods. But he instead stumbled upon online internet marketing and embarked on an unconventional route to becoming an internet millionaire. It was not an easy route, because he had to juggle learning about the new internet marketing model of which he knew nothing about while still working a full-time job. But his burning desire to be rich got him through the hurdle and eventually to financial freedom.

Start to imagine yourself as already having wealth. Before you physically acquire the wealth that you have envisioned, you need to own it as if you already possess the amount of money that you desire! In other words, how would you feel right now if you were wealthy? What would you be doing differently? How would your life be different? How would your day unfold? Start to "own" the result of your wealth now! Here's why. The subconscious mind is unable to differentiate between actual possession and mere visualization. So, by imagining that you already have it, you are encouraging your subconscious mind to seek ways to transform your imaginary feelings into the real thing. I know many people refute this type of thinking as impractical. But if you think about it, isn't everything around us a true manifestation of someone else's imagination? Everything man made was in someone's imagination before it was created. And when they possessed the passion to create it, the ways and means appeared. The wright brothers imagined being able to fly, and the reality is, we are now able to fly in an airplane from one country to another in a matter of hours. And it didn't happen with their first trial.

I recently flew on an 880 Air Bus from San Francisco to Dubai. It holds almost 700 passengers and the wingspan is 30 feet shy of the length of a football field. I'll bet with Wright brothers would be impressed.

Thomas Edison imagined lighting a whole room using a single source, and as a result, the light bulb was invented! Yes, it took a few tries, about 10,000, but eventually he created it, and now it lights the world.

Look around right now. If you are in a room, look at all the things in that room that made someone wealthy. Why not you? Take a walk outside and look around. How many things do you see that made some else wealthy? Why not you? It all started in someone's imagination. They owned it first in their mind and heart before it became a reality. It's a fact that without the imagination of great visionaries, we would not be able to enjoy many things that we enjoy today. Refrigerators, radio, television, automobiles, cell phones and thousands of other great inventions we would not enjoy today if not for someone first imagining it into existence.

Decision comes first, then the answers! You too possess the same capability to create, improve your own destiny by constructing it in your mind first. All improvement in your life begins in the improvement of your mental pictures. Change your mental pictures and you change the outcome of your life, like changing a movie on TV. For example, you can imagine receiving income checks when you open the mailbox every day. Or you can picture yourself receiving an award for being nominated the best entrepreneur in your country or having a best-selling book. Not only does it send the message to your subconscious, it serves as a great form of daily inspiration.

It is absolutely essential to have a crystal-clear picture of what you want to accomplish before you begin. If you want to attain wealth you must learn to operate with a sharply defined mental image of the outcome you want to attain. Focus your attention on the spot where you want to land, not on where you are now, or on any misconceptions or shortcomings you may think you have. In other words, visualize your arrival and you will develop a magnetic harmony with the ways and means required to get there. Solutions will begin to appear, and obstacles will seem to disappear. Answers will come to you. People will show up to support you in your endeavor.

Look at the end result as something that you are already prepared to do, you just haven't done it yet. Think about this. Your success is something that you have been preventing, it is not something you have to struggle to make happen.

You'll find the solutions taking you toward your goals will come to you in the most unexpected and sudden ways when you let go of the old you, reinvent a new you, and embrace your new money philosophy. You don't need the *perfect* plan first. What you need is a *perfectly* clear decision about your success, the right mindset, and the ideal way to get you there will materialize. You can't get all the answers up front so don't waste your time trying. The success formula doesn't involve getting everything neatly organized, with everything in its proper place and sequence and all the risks eliminated before you make the move. If you want that, then get a 9-5 job, but realize that will never make you wealthy. Get a target…point, then take action! Your true greatness lies within your ability to decide what you want and commitment to having it, and then taking bold action to get it.

The world you have visualized in the past is the world you now live in. The world you visualize now is the world you will create in the future. And the world you create is limited only by your imagination, your mindset, and your ability to let go of the old beliefs that keep you stuck and reinvent the new you.

Everyone has the right to be wealthy. You have the right to be wealthy. Yet, most allow a temporary lack of money to eat into their minds, literally confining them into the vicious cycle of mediocrity. The bottom line is that people are poor because they have not yet decided to be rich.

So long as you make a conscious decision to become wealthy and have the utmost faith that you can achieve it, you will always act accordingly to what you believe. We create our own reality either unconsciously without purpose or consciously with a purpose. A person who believes that the universe is abundant and they can attain whatever level of financial success they desire…and a person who believes that money only comes from working hard and will receive money only from hard work…are both right. Each will have many experiences to prove that their belief about abundance is a fact. The good news is though…you can change your belief and therefore change your experience. Change your money philosophy and you will change the amount of money flowing to you. This same philosophy applies to any area of your life. What you resonate with is what you will create, and with 100% accuracy

***

To contact Jim:

www.jimbritt.com

www.jimbrittcoaching.com

www.facebook.com/jimbrittonline

www.linkedin.com/in/jim-britt

Kevin Harrington

Kevin Harrington is an original shark from the hit TV show *Shark Tank* and a successful entrepreneur for more than forty years. He's the co-founding board member of the Entrepreneurs' Organization and co-founder of the Electronic Retailing Association. He also invented the infomercial. He helped make "But wait... There's more!" part of our cultural history. He's one of the pioneers behind the *As Seen on TV* brand, has heard more than 50,000 pitches, and launched more than 500 products generating more than $5 Billion in global sales. Twenty of his companies have generated more than $100 million in revenue each. He's also the founder of the *Secrets of Closing the Sale Master Class* inspired by the Master of sales—Zig Ziglar. He's the author of several bestselling books including *Act Now: How I Turn Ideas into Million Dollar Products, Key Person of Influence,* and *Put a Shark in Your Tank.*

Becoming A KPI

By Kevin Harrington

The Key Person of Influence (KPI) in any given industry is the leader. It is the leader of the business world, the leader of automobile dealerships, the leader of selling hats—you name it. In other words, being the KPI means being the go-to person. The crazy thing? Anyone can be a Key Person of Influence. Any entrepreneur can be a KPI, a doctor, a salesperson, anyone. Just follow five steps and you will be well on your way. What comes with being a Key Person of Influence is value, ideally a massive amount of money, and being the leader in your field. The KPI is the person who comes up in conversations when it relates to a certain product, business, company, industry, or field. This is the person others seek out, the go-to person. Being the Key Person of Influence is how I got on *Shark Tank*.

Here's the story: I got a phone call from Mark Burnett's company. Mark Burnett is a television producer. He produced shows like *Survivor* and *The Voice*. His office called to set up an appointment. Mark was starting up a new show and wanted me to go out to Los Angeles to talk business. I was curious as to how Mark Burnett's company found me, and why they reached out for my services. They told me it was because I was a Key Person of Influence. I was all over the internet as a result of everything I was doing. It was 2008, and I had been in the business for 25 years. I had created huge brands. I helped build Tony Little. I helped build Jack Lalanne. I helped build Food Saver. We did the NuWave Oven. We worked with people like George Foreman and countless others. The problem was, everybody knew the brands, which was good for business, but did nothing for my personal brand. Consumers knew about the Food Saver, they knew about Tony Little, and they knew about Jack Lalanne, but not everyone knew I was the guy behind all of these people. Nobody knew me.

At that point, I made a conscious effort to build my brand. I wanted to become the go-to person so I could get the hot products and the phone calls. I helped build Tony Little's business, but everyone called him; they weren't calling me. What's wrong with that picture? Well, for one, I invested millions and millions of dollars of my own capital into Tony Little, and then he got all the phone calls. Shame on me for doing that, right? So, I decided to build my brand, and that's when I came out with my book, *Key Person of Influence*. I promoted myself by doing radio talk shows, TV shows, trade journals, speeches, etc. This is how I got on *Shark Tank*.

If I hadn't met Daniel Priestley, my book could have become *How To Become The Go-To Guy* because that's what I was looking to do, but Daniel very eloquently created this five-step system called the "Key Person of Influence." Realizing we were on to something, we co-authored and launched *Key Person of Influence*. Let's look now at the necessary steps to become a KPI.

Obtaining Customers

In 1984, I started a business of obtaining customers on TV. One evening, I was watching the Discovery Channel and suddenly the channel went dark for about six hours. I then called the cable company just in case there was a problem. They told me there wasn't a problem, that the Discovery Channel was an 18-hour network. That's when the light bulb went off. This was downtime. They put no value on those six down hours. Instead of showing something during this time, bars were put up on the screen. I started thinking about what I could put in place of that downtime, to sell something, obtain customers, and make money. I'm like the Rembrandt TV guy. I created and invented the whole concept of going to TV stations and buying huge blocks of remnant downtime. In all these years of me doing this, no one has challenged the idea that I was the person who did it, created it, and invented 30-minute infomercial blocks.

I was buying big blocks of time. Why? Because I wanted to obtain customers. How do you obtain customers? A lot of ways, but you ultimately have to get some form of media. How does it start? There are two metrics you have to look at when obtaining customers. What does it cost to obtain the customer? That is called the Cost Per Order (CPO). What is your Average Lifetime Revenue Value (ALRV), or Average Order Value (AOV)? The cost to obtain the customer obviously has to be less than the cost you are going to receive in income from the customer. The bottom line in obtaining customers: you have to set up a system. You have to set up testing. You have to set up as many sources for obtaining customers as possible. Even though I was in the TV business, I didn't just get customers through TV. Customers came through TV, radio, the internet, retail stores, international distribution, home shopping channels, etc. The first step is to make a laundry list of every possible resource for attracting these customers.

Today, some people who are into the digital space are basically just getting customers on the internet. Some of the areas I mentioned above have become very expensive. It's tougher to make money on TV. While we started on TV, the cost to get customers has become too high; so we now have made the switch to digital. When you talk about internet, there's many different ways to obtain customers, from Google AdWords to Facebook ads to social media, etc. You can also attain customers with public relations and influencers. You have to decide what works best with your product. The bottom line is a lot of people do not realize they have to be sophisticated, from a business analysis standpoint, to set up a business. You need a marketing plan to obtain customers.

First, focus on two numbers: your Customer Acquisition Cost (CAT) and Average Order Value (AOV). Those numbers have to work. Customer service is crucial in the business world as well. A business can't have bad customer service and retain customers This is especially true in this day-and-age.

Raising Capital

I had a 50-million-dollar-a-year business, making $5 million a year in profit. Feeling confident, I met with seven banks to get some financing. I thought it was going to be easy because I had a very profitable business. Unfortunately, bank after bank after bank turned me down. I had great credit and all of that. The only asset I had was the business. Part of the problem was I didn't know how to approach the banks. I was a young entrepreneur in my twenties. I had no real credibility in the banking world; I was walking in and just showing my numbers from the year before.

So, what did I do to get the capital? Well, I ran into a mentor who was a former bank president, and he said, "Kevin, you went about it all wrong. I come from the banking business, and if you walked into my office and said, 'I need 5 million bucks,' I would have told you to turn around and get the hell out of my office. What do you have to do? You have to sell them on the future. What you did last year is well and good, but they are giving you money because they know that you are still going to be in business three years from now repaying their loans. You need projections. You need your forward business plan. You need your five-year master plan. You need to talk the talk and walk the walk, otherwise they aren't even interested."

I hired my mentor as a consultant to the company. I brought him in on the ground floor as part of my dream team. To make a long story short, we went back to re-pitch some of the same banks. We didn't get 5 million dollars, but we got a 3-million-dollar line of credit. It was all in how we talked to the banks. We had the same business, but it was all in the presentation. It's all in how you talk and how prepared you are. Raising capital is mental. It's in the pitch. It's in the relationships you build, etc.

One of the biggest challenges with any business is having enough capital to do the things you want to do. You have to have a successful business plan if you want to raise money. Here are the elements of a successful business plan.

> (1) You need an executive summary (one page summarizing the whole plan). You need an industry overview, defining the problem you are solving and an overview of the market.
>
> (2) You need a description of your product or the service. How does it serve as a solution?
>
> (3) You need a competitive analysis. What/who is your competition?
>
> (4) You need a sales and marketing plan.
>
> (5) You need to identify your target customer and proof for your concept.

(6) What is your method of operations?

(7) Who's on your management team, your board of advisers, your dream team?

(8) What are your financial projections?

(9) You need to outline your risk analysis and appendix.

If you are going to raise capital, you don't just talk to an investor. I get people all the time that come to me saying they have an idea, and boom… it's on a napkin. They tell me that they just need $100K for 10 percent. I ask if they can send me their business plan. They then ask me what I mean when I say, 'business plan.' If they don't have one, that means I am going to end up giving them 100K and never see it again.

One of the most important parts of raising capital is coming up with a reasonable ask, and then explaining how the proceeds will be used. Many entrepreneurs don't understand this. For example, a guy came on *Shark Tank* saying he needed 150K for 10 percent of his company. I asked what he was going to use the 150K for?

His response was essentially this, "Well, I am going to use the money as a down payment for a piece of real estate where we are going to build a building, then launch the business."

"Okay, so you are going to build the building and then equip the building with furniture. Where is that money going to come from?" I asked. He said once he got the real estate, then they would figure out that batch of money at that time. I told him, "$150K dollars doesn't get you in business. $150K dollars gets you a piece of land. How are you going to build the business, generate revenue, and pay me back?" This guy told me he thought I would have more money for him after that. I said, "Well, no. You are not going to get the first batch of money based on the answers you are giving me."

Instead, he should have said he was going to lease a small office and start generating massive amounts of revenue with the money I gave them. Then, pay me back all of my money, plus a huge return on my investment, and then build it into a global business. That's what I wanted to hear. I want to know that people have a successful business plan, a successful marketing plan, and then I will talk about how to go about raising the capital, how to call on investors, and what the sweet spots are for the investors.

The bottom line on raising capital is, you can't just go build yourself a huge global business without thinking about how you're going to finance it. In the old days, I thought if I built a successful business, money was going to be easy. It's not, unless you know how to do it. There's an art to raising capital. Part of it involves making sure you are prepared and know how to pitch your business properly.

The Perfect Pitch

While the actual product or service you are trying to sell is a critical part of the process, it is just as important to sell the customer on yourself, your services, and your business. Even though I have made thousands upon thousands of pitches, have spoken to thousands of people, and have seen a great amount of success, I still pitch myself and my businesses. No matter who you are, or what you do, you have to be ready to drop the perfect pitch. It doesn't matter if you are going to make this perfect pitch in front of a crowd of thousands, or a crowd of one. To help with the concept of a perfect pitch, I have created a 10-step system.

Before you can start perfecting the perfect pitch, you have to ask yourself a couple of questions. What are you pitching? In other words, what product, business, or service are you trying to sell? Next, what do you want to get out of this pitch? More customers? More sales? Nonetheless, these questions are for you to answer, and you need to answer them before devising your perfect pitch. The perfect pitch can be broken down into these 10 steps:

(1) The **Tease** is your hook; the period of time when you plant the seed. This is when you reveal a problem. You have to explain to your customers why you are giving the pitch. You also have to use showmanship, which sets the pace for the rest of the pitch. If your showmanship skills are demonstrated in the Tease portion of your pitch, then you will have your audience (or your customer) hooked from the very beginning.

(2) Next up is **Please**. In this part of the perfect pitch, you are telling your customer how your product or service can solve the problem you mapped out in the first step. Ideally, your product or service will solve this stated problem in the most efficient, elegant, and cost-effective way. You have to relay to your customer that your solution is the best solution, and it will solve the problem better than anything (or anyone) else. It is important to also show off your features and benefits, and to display the magical transformation that will take place.

(3) The third step to the perfect pitch is **Demonstration/Multi-functionality**. First, you have to ask yourself if you can demonstrate your product, your service and your value. This is the key to any successful pitch, and it brings multi-functionality to the forefront. It shows it off. Think of this step as an added value. Ideally, your service or product is multifunctional. If you can show this off to your customer, then you just brought bonus points to the table.

(4) But Wait There's More! is the fourth step, and it's not just for infomercials on TV. This is the step where you give more value to your product or service by showing and adding more to the pitch—maybe added bonus items or "buy 2 get 1 free if you act now" incentives. At this point, your customer should already be biting, but now is the time to really win them over. So, show them what else you have to offer.

(5) Testimonials are the fifth step to creating the perfect pitch. You are now using someone else to do the pitching. In other words, who says so besides you? This is the proof behind your business, product, or service. Testimonials can include consumers (actual users of the product or service), professionals (leaders in your industry), editorial (articles, experts, press, journals, trade publications, magazines, newspapers), etc. Testimonials can also feature celebrities. Celebrity testimonials can be very powerful for the simple fact that people love celebrities. Then there are documented testimonials, which can include clinical studies, labs tests, and science. Once again, this is one of the most important areas for creating the perfect pitch.

(6) Another important step is **Research and Competitive Analysis**. For this step, you should be asking yourself if you have done your research. If so, then this is the portion of the perfect pitch when you show off all of that information. This can include information on the industry, market and competitors. It can also be facts, figures, and statistics. This research should show off the fact that you, your company, and your product/service is unique.

(7) The seventh step is **Your Team.** In this step, you are bringing the credibility of your team and putting it right there on the metaphorical table. Who makes up your team? It could be advisers, management, directors, and strategic partners. Your team will help scale, open connections, add on the knowledge factor, and so much more.

(8) Why? is the eighth step. Why are you pitching? How will the person in front of you help? This step will change based on who you are actually pitching to. For example, if you are looking for funds, then this is a big section, and you need to incorporate many talking points.

(9) The ninth step is **Marketing Plan.** You have done your pitch and given out all your information. Now, how will you make everything happen? For instance, you need to know your marketing and distribution plan. As is the case throughout your entire pitch, it is essential that you show confidence. Sell whoever you are pitching on your product or service, and yourself as well. People invest in people all the time.

(10) The 10th and final step is **Seize**. You laid everything out, now ask! What are you trying to accomplish? Ask it! Being the final step, this is the time to present the final call to action.

Remember, each pitch will be different. Some pitches last for over an hour and others last only a few seconds or minutes. It just depends on how much time you are given or how much time you need. That is why you need to craft your pitches accordingly. Practice, practice, and more practice.

***

To contact Kevin:

www.KevinHarrington.tv

Noah Amparano

Noah Amparano is a student of life. His mission is to help create and inspire a different possibility in the lives around him. He has overcome multiple learning and educational challenges with such ease that it shocks people to this very day. In his work life, he has gone from professional athlete, to international fashion model, to business owner. He has found that anything is possible when you have a willingness to be aggressively present in your life, ask the right questions and choose to be more than you already are.

It's Just a Choice

By Noah Amparano

I don't often share my story with people, but when Jim asked me to write a chapter in this book, I couldn't think of a better way to share my experiences and lessons that I have gained in my years as an entrepreneur and performance coach.

I have found that the stories we tell ourselves can change the direction of our lives and the lives of those around us.

When I was 6 years old growing up in Napa, Calif., I realized that I wasn't like my fellow classmates. While my friends around me were learning to read and write, I couldn't make sense of the letters and struggled with completing assignments.

My lack of cooperation was interpreted as acting out. I was not making progress and my teachers became frustrated. My mom did some research and found a learning center in Houston, Texas, where I went to be assessed.

They hooked me up to different machines and put me through series of tests—auditory, graph, visual and brain scans.

They tested me every day, and when they couldn't figure out what was wrong with me, they sat me down in a chair and said, "You're never going to be able to read or write or be able to function in society."

I never told my parents that this was said to me, but years later, I told them, and it was confirmed by the learning center. They claimed, in their "professional opinion," that their assessments of me were correct.

From the ages of about 6 to 10 years old, I traveled to at least eight different schools in Texas, Illinois, Arizona and California, as my family tried to find help for me. My mom, my older brother and I lived in a series of motels while my dad stayed back in Napa, working.

I attended another school in Corte Madera, Calif., where they customized each student's learning program. It seemed more structured, but for me it was like trying to put a puzzle together with different pieces. I was also put on a series of stimulants, which helped my concentration, but then made things worse.

I had terrible rages in the middle of the night, where I would see severed limbs coming at me and I'd be swinging my arms and hitting my mom as she tried to wake me up. Doctors prescribed a variety of medicines: Depakote, Seroquel, Lithium, Albuterol and other heavy-duty drugs.

The rages alternated with periods of mania and depression. I was diagnosed with bipolar disorder and was taken to Stanford University, where they took me off of stimulants and gave me strong antidepressants in the hope my moods would stabilize.

For a while, it was quiet, but my terrible rages came back. My mom carried paper bags everywhere we went. I would breathe into them whenever I started to have a panic attack. Sometimes when we would be driving on the freeway, I would feel so overwhelmed that I would try to open the car door while we were moving at 60 miles an hour. My brother and my mom would grab the seatbelt and pull me back in.

My action was interpreted as a suicide attempt, but to me, I was just trying to escape.

One summer day, when I was about 12, I had a panic attack and nearly drowned.

My mom would sometimes drop off my brother and I so we could go swimming at my auntie's house. While I was swimming, I had a panic attack and started gasping and swallowing water, ending up at the bottom of the pool. My aunt saw me and raced to pull me out.

The next thing I remembered was waking up in what looked like a dorm room, and I had no clue about how I got there. I was in a room with a stranger I had never met.

None of my family was around. I was there alone; I remember walking out through two steel doors to a front desk, asking "Where is my mom?" I was told I was brought there because I had tried to kill myself. I remember feeling this pain and loneliness. I felt like I had this hole in my chest.

Here at this treatment center, though, I noticed I was not alone in facing challenges. I saw people with difficult situations—who had no families, no direction in their lives or any kind of program that seemed to work for them.

Gradually, I experienced a shift. I started helping others to become aware that they can choose something greater. Sometimes I would help out the staff or I would talk to someone having a bad day. I would also share my food with kids whose families couldn't bring them anything.

The staff brought me in to talk to the board. They said, "Why are you here? You don't belong here." In all the years they'd had patients, they hadn't seen anyone who did what I did. The other kids changed; the energy was different every day.

When I got out, another school awaited. They studied the ways I learned. This introduced me to a totally different way of functioning in the world. I tried things that I felt might work, I responded, and tailored the methods accordingly. It didn't matter whether I needed to learn how to read. It didn't matter if I took the SAT. My learning was based on experiencing the real world.

In later years, assessments showed that I was not bipolar, as earlier diagnosed. I began teaching myself how to read and write at the age of 12. I remember starting to look at road signs and freeway traffic signs as a way to become familiar with words. I started to notice words all around me and began using the "real world" as my library. I soon transitioned to social media and journaling about my business ideas and putting creative thoughts down on paper.

I wanted to give back in some way, I decided to teach at Star Academy in San Rafael, Calif., a school for special needs kids that helped me as a teen. I volunteered helping kids with motor skills, balance and learning. I was invited into the classrooms to share my story. I wanted to give back to kids who struggled like I did. I wanted them to choose a life of purpose and direction that they could follow, using tools that they could adapt to any environment. When they would "get" something I was teaching, it made my day. It was so cool, so rewarding.

In this chapter, I am sharing the tools that I have used to change my direction in life.

What I have found from being around people who have truly created major success for themselves is that they are honest and have clarity about their choices.

In my own life, asking questions has empowered me to be aware of what is actually possible and the choices that are available.

When you ask the question, you have to be willing to get the energy of what you want; you don't always have to have a fixed point of view of what it's going to look like.

I found that the art of asking questions is probably the No. 1 most important skill you can master because it offers a way to live in the present moment. For anyone trying to create more possibility, it's good to know that something more is out there; to create an awareness to see the choices that are available.

I have always pushed myself to look at how I can do more and be more, and never be satisfied with what I have done for others and for myself. What we choose is not wrong; it's just a choice.

When I started to make a real change in my life, I asked one very simple yet powerful question: **What actions can I take today to create the future I would like to have tomorrow?**

It was as if my world flipped like an hourglass and the sand poured as an infinite source of possibilities.

I started asking questions when things didn't go as planned or when something unexpected happened. This didn't slow or stop my momentum; it actually opened me up and continued to create more space in my life.

After a childhood in which I was always perceived to be wrong about something, now I was finally free to create the life I desired.

This doesn't just apply to work or business. You have to think: How would you like to be in the world? How would you like to be seen in the world? What kind of presence would you like to have in any hour of the day?

I started living by faith, not by sight.

When I tell people these stories, they look at me and can't understand how questions can have such an impact on someone's life. I always express to them that the questions allow you to be present without needing to make a forceful reaction to a particular situation that takes you away from the present moment.

Getting you back to the present moment is about not having an expectation. You have to be willing to receive everything good or bad and whatever comes your way.

I ask people this question: When someone cuts you off when you are on the freeway, do you get angry? Do you want to get back at the person for what he did? All you're focused on is a reaction, which stops you from receiving.

I remember when I would drive from Marin to Napa Valley in the late afternoon and I would see these amazing sunsets. I thought: **How does it get any better than this?** Sunsets bring a different energy, but it's a gradual energy. The sun has to set gradually, and then rise gradually.

If you react to anger, you start to align and agree, and you take that energy out of what you would actually like to create. You're like a steaming pot on a stove. What if, instead, you asked: How does it get any better than this?

When you do this, you're telling the situation to become better. It changes your emotional state.

You're inviting something greater to occur and not reacting to the trauma and drama being projected at you. You're coming from a different place of being willing to receive something greater.

I have used multiple processes and questions throughout my career to help create some incredible experiences—not just for myself, but for my athletes, students, and businesses. In addition to the long process of overcoming my learning challenges, I have had some fun adventures along the way—including traveling as an international fashion model and dining with royalty in Thailand.

I found that when you stay in the question, you create the energy you would like to have in your life.

Staying in the question helps you see that no matter what you go through, you're not defined by what people tell you. It's a lot easier to listen to your own truth, your own voice.

When people say that you can't do something, and you listen to them, you're saying that their voice is more important than yours. If you just realize that it's white noise, you start to develop your own voice.

I feel strongly about this because I had to not only find my voice; I had to create my own voice. I had to modify the tone and I had to listen to what was being said to me inside before I could start changing the outside of what I wanted to create.

I believe in developing and creating your own internal dialogue, and sometimes that requires you to recognize that people are telling you negative things. I look at this analogy in a couple of ways.

You have two pies. One is a dirt pie and one is a cherry pie. When people judge you or project a limiting or negative point of view at you, I say, "Thanks for the dirt pie." I take it and I put it aside, and then I take the cherry pie instead. People will try to feed you dirt pies and you have the choice to eat that dirt pie or not.

You have the choice to set that dirt pie down and say, "I'm going to eat this cherry pie instead and I'm going to enjoy it."

A great way to practice this exercise is to hold your hands out in front of you whenever you feel like you are being offered a dirt pie and say to yourself "thank for the dirt pie" and then set it aside. Try it and see how you feel next time someone tries to project their own limiting points of view on your life.

I have found through my experience that **"no momentum is bad momentum,"** and that people have the keys to their own success.

I remember one time when I was depressed after a breakup, and I was standing at my bathroom sink. It felt like my feet were stuck in bubble gum. I was lost in my own thoughts. I left the house and went for a drive. It made me realize you need to keep moving.

I grew up in a harsh environment at a young age. I had to be a light for myself. Even though I couldn't see it, I had to make sure that inside me there was still some type of light. In times of crisis and panic, there is great opportunity if you can see it.

In my coaching work, I have clients who want to stop instantly when they encounter a roadblock. *"If I am doing something that doesn't serve me, why should I do it? Isn't that considered bad momentum?"*

It's more about how it is serving your vision that you have for your life and your future, as well as how that can be a contribution to others.

It's your point of view that needs to change about what you are doing, then your situation will change. If you are not doing anything to consistently improve yourself or your situation, then how can you expect your circumstance to change?

What you think, you will attract, and what you think, you will become.

When you make the conscious choice to change, you change and then so do the plants, animals and people around you.

For instance, when I go fishing, before I go out, I ask for the plants and animals around me to contribute, and I have not missed a fish on those days. When you ask, you start to change the energy, the molecules: I'm committing to this, choosing this. Please help. You step up and everything around you wants to contribute to you. The environment creates with you, not against you.

When I was just getting out of high school, I came to an awareness that I wanted more out of life.

I had lots of energy but didn't have a clear direction of where I wanted to take it. I knew that I needed to make a choice in order to start creating what I would actually like to have show up in my life.

Over the next few weeks, I went around asking friends and family what they did to live a fuller life. I tried everything imaginable, from sparking conversations up with random people in stores, to asking other strangers what they did for a living and how their choices led them to where they are today.

Taking in this information, I asked myself: What will my life be like in five years if I choose this? And what will my life be like in five years if I don't choose this?

This question is truly a game-changer because you are creating your life every single day by the choices you make. This will save energy and time as you create your future. I have used this in times when I found myself second-guessing a big choice or opportunity… if what I was about to choose was really for me. It has been an incredible asset/tool to keep me on track and to have the confidence and self-assurance that my choice is creating the life I really would like to have.

How many times have you had a thought or a feeling about something or someone that you found yourself getting stuck with and it kept repeating itself over and over again?

For example, have you felt like someone was silently judging you? Or there was a particular incident that involved you, but you perceived the worst possibility and that made things worse, based on your thoughts, feelings or emotions?

Have you ever heard that saying "everything is not what it appears to be"?

It's exactly true. Most of the time we let our thoughts, feelings, and emotions do that talking without really taking a step back and becoming aware of what we are actually perceiving to be true.

When you choose awareness over your thoughts, feelings, and emotions, you take back the control over your emotional world. You're allowing yourself a sense of freedom, so you don't have to suffer with the trauma and drama. You allow yourself to be present with what's in front of you, as you ask yourself, **"What's right about this that I'm not getting?"**

You're not allowing yourself to get stuck. You're allowing yourself to receive something greater by not having a set point of view. There could be something more than what's in front of you. This starts to develop an optimistic mindset because you're willing to really create from a space that works for you.

It's important for anyone who wants to have more freedom to develop a more positive mindset to understand that thoughts, feelings and emotions are just that, nothing more and nothing less.

When you understand this, it makes managing your energy that much easier.

Here is a question that helps create awareness of what is actually true when you find yourself reeling from thoughts, feelings and emotions.

What's right about this that I am not getting? Interesting point of view—I have this point of view.

When you function from the question and everything is just an interesting point of view, there is no room for the trauma and drama or limitation; there is only clarity of what is and what is actually possible.

We all have a unique capacity of picking up on other peoples' energy, and when we have to manage ours on top of that, it can feel like their energy is our own. This is where people can get depressed and inflict harm on themselves or others.

I have found through my practice that this question ("What's right about this…") has allowed me, throughout my life, to manage times of depression or negativity. It has moved me toward better choices a lot faster than sitting with negative thoughts that marinate in my head.

We are all capable of such beauty and compassion for each other and I think it's time we harness this power to choose this presence for ourselves.

These questions and tools have helped me through some of the darkest times in my life and have contributed to a kindness that I now have for myself and my work today.

This book has been an absolute delight to contribute to; if there was anything that you take away from this chapter, I hope it is that there are always different possibilities and choices available.

Remember, it's not right or wrong; it is just a choice.

***

To contact Noah:

Instagram: https://www.instagram.com/noahamp/

LinkedIn: https://www.linkedin.com/in/noah-amparano-641481b0/

Twitter: https://twitter.com/noah_amparano

Kendra Steel

"Dark Horse Coach" of the community, and owner of Becoming Alpha, Kendra Steel's versatility ranges from business to metaphysical. She credits reading poetry in the community of Everett for furthering her passion towards personal growth and self-exploration, leading her down the path of improving lives worldwide.

She began coaching in 2016 with ideals influenced by the powerhouses, Tony Robbins and Marie Forleo, aside her full-time aerospace machinist job in Washington state.

Once known as "lost cause," now Life Coach, Kendra has proven an unwavering level of integrity for her fellow coaches to live up to. Her art to coaching has shown her clients what truly living in splendor in all areas of your life can look like, and she continuously preaches what she learned from the team at Recalibrate 360: "Everyone is doing the very best they can with the tools they have available to them at the time." She has since lived a message of commitment and strength for herself, and her clients, all of which now found amidst highly fulfilled endeavors.

As a Native Paiute woman, Kendra is dedicating her journey and the gifts she utilizes with others, to the peoples of the original tribes of the world. Her mission is to use these gifts to restore their way of living, one client, or many, at a time."

Pandemic to Prosperous

By Kendra Steel

Before this chapter begins, I need to set the scene for you. In any story the background is more important than we give it credit for, and to think this time is any different would be fatal to what you could potentially gain from it.

As of spring, 2020, Covid-19, or the Corona Virus, has become a very familiar story to just about anyone on the planet anymore. It's become the second guess work in everything we do as of now.

You should also keep in mind that before I submitted this chapter I had a whole array of words conjured up for you based on perseverance, overcoming your own inner dialogue, and making your stay on this planet memorable for more than just yourself. This outline is still fairly similar, but the purpose and the root cause was changed the moment the governor of Washington, where I'm from, issued a stay-at-home order for the entire state. Was my business in jeopardy? A cautious side of me always prepares. But, preparation and actually running through the motions are only comparable, which is why Kenny Rogers keeps playing in my head nowadays. "Knowing when to hold 'em" in a pandemic has become a tool worth putting in your back pocket.

The first instinct I had, hearing it for the first time at work (and being as I was the only woman in the pool of male machinists at the time) was to laugh about how the virus was correlated to the popular beer.

However, I knew, just like you know when you should look both ways before crossing a railroad, (just in case your ears falsified the train horn for white noise) this was going to become...something. Not just in physical relationships, but in my business.

Just the inkling of why this moment felt so significant made me pause my jokes and let the "other guys" step in for their spotlight. Being a machinist, practicing Life Coach, was shifting my head different ways from where it had been for quite some time, (let's say, alienated from the reality and professionalism of starting a professional business) and as anything switches paths, it kept my caution from the wind and made me ponder over my next set of choices.

Everything was a joke to us. Even the things you should really keep on lock and key in your own mind, if that. About two weeks after, on January 31st I left the machining world after eight years in the aerospace industry to practice Coaching full time.

Between then and today, I had roughly two and a half months to really submerge myself in the field of working from home, marketing from scratch, and keeping my head above water amidst the lingering sanity from too much freedom. From then until just a few weeks ago, jokes became the saboteur, and I eventually lost a bit of my humor, which I used to consider the key to my own kingdom. I became the struggling artist, and my art was coaching people to become their best selves. Regardless of how abundant I was, and how passionate I was about the outcomes I was helping create, my scarcity mindset was adjacent to a new mentality I never imagined I would inherit: the "who am I to..." mentality. I had my own demons sitting on my shoulder, as I'm sure you do now.

Fast forward to today, and here I sit, rewriting my chapter based off the sole idea that right now, there is a major deficit in leaders. Since before the outbreak, I've had a lingering question, which I feel has become more vital to answer now more than ever: How do we become leaders, thereby more equipped to pick the right ones? The answer, less apparent, is we become them. (And not the kind of leader you make yourself out to be to your kids before wallowing in self-pity when they finally go to sleep) I mean the kind of hero that celebrates even the smallest accomplishments with the highest chin, because those are the wins that equate to the final step on the Mt. Everest challenges of starting and maintaining a business. Keep in mind, this can start in a business and seep into every realm of your life. Dedication and passion are chameleons.

So, I decided, if this chapter is to be about "cracking my own rich code" then it needs to be about how I cracked my own shell and re-birthed myself into a new world practically formed on uncertainty and the scarcity mindset, but also optimism and dedication. More so, it needs to be about how you can learn along the same ideas, whether you relate to my story or not.

Working from home as a self-made entrepreneur is where you'll find even the scariest forms of obstacles. They deal with inner turmoil, or inner dialogues that have been quieted for so long, hearing them speak again is like reading legal jargon for the first time. Not only is it confusing, but the idea that you might miss something crucial is almost terrifying.

So, as you read this next part, I wonder if it would be possible to really sink yourself into the scenery. That is, a collapsing economy, a will to work without resources, and a plethora of "reasons" why depression and procrastination are the proper scapegoat when you still have a business to run.

The purpose? To really understand the only thing stopping you is what you tell yourself.

(Also, maybe a bit of taking responsibility. That part is optional.)

So, there we were put, on the border that separated chaos itself, and the opportunity to use our skills to transform our lives from the inside out. (Literally, inside our own homes.) The choice to choose one or the other had never been more obvious, albeit significant.

Some decided to judge their progress based on their neighbors, while the rest sank or swam in their own kiddie pools; strategically placed in their living rooms.

The necessity to connect was grossly underestimated by the planet when it was abruptly taken away. A panic induced from mass lay-offs enhanced the worldwide scarcity factor. The story based off of one global circumstance had the markings of almost every Stephen King novel, and it was scary to most of us, the idea we could finally relate to them.

If someone were to ask the millions, if not billions of people effected "what's in a virus?" the answer would be drastically expanded post 2020. The amount who would correlate this virus to maintaining their business would be a pitiful number.

If ever before there was a time to grow a business, the moment had long passed with no light to show us when the reprieve would end.

However, the code we forged within ourselves was what we used to succeed (those of us who took this as another trial to prove our resilience). It was the time to acknowledge every bit of the "I can, I will, I must" talk we practiced months, years, and decades before. Was it time to question whether or not we could? Was it an opportunity to dwell on the answer? For some, sure. But, more so, we as entrepreneurs understand this question as past tense - "of course we can" is always the answer, and we use it as a propeller to move forward.

We live in a very uncertain world. A global crisis has a brilliant trait of being spontaneous. As an eternal student, which, in my humble opinion, would be a brilliant definition of "entrepreneur," it is our job to walk on stones across a roaring river, balancing chaos in one hand and solutions in the other.

The bottom line, regardless of the *external dialogue, is this: if you truly want to succeed, you will. Pandemic, or slow month, you *will find the loopholes in what appears to be a hopeless situation if you truly want to utilize your potential and become Limitless.

A learning situation like this offers a glimpse into a new level of understanding. It provides the steps, the map, and the obstacles. Your task is to find the source of your weakness that holds you back from climbing the staircase and acknowledge it for what it is. Is it a program you've incorporated into your psyche? Or is it a habit you've created out of comfort, regardless of what it's kept you from? Keep in mind, there is no good or bad here, it's just what is, and now you have a chance to take it out of your timeline.

Are you willing to do the work?

The next step is allowing complete and utter honesty with yourself as you ask the next questions:

"Am I ready to learn?"

"Am I ready to take responsibility for how I handled this weakness?"

"How far will my dedication, right now, for this business take me?"

You can find, on an unconscious level, what is holding you back with ease. It's the part where you take control and throw it out of your life that so many of us seem to struggle with.

With that being said, have you ever noticed that the times of struggle are when you hear the harsh criticism the most? Would you consider me insane if I told you those voices are the tools, almost catalysts, to a brighter future? Imagine, if you would, you, as an entrepreneur, are trying to untie the knot which halted your income. You not only have something to prove to the world, but to yourself. You're geared towards pleasure; the idea of becoming highly successful, even in a drastic state of the country. You hear external dialogue, and now your own has finally succumbed to them as well. Every voice you hear is a repetition of the last, giving you reasons why settling for a random day job instead of keeping your business is the best, safest idea. What do you do?

Criticism is always the knife sharpener. There is a wide array of ways to transform criticism from a blow to the throat to a helpful step up the mountain. My biggest critic, myself, was about one thousand times harsher than my most intimidating critic, my former boss.

Enter, Fred Schule, The Gordon Ramsey of the machining world. He may not ever read this, but if he does, it will be partially because at one point in time, I felt more compelled to prove him wrong about something than to let him think I couldn't do it, whatever "it" was. As far as building a business, take my words heavily when I say this was the man to learn from, so his criticism in any area was a harsh reality check, regardless of what it was directed towards. Machining was his forte, and I was bold enough to make Life Coaching mine. However, I was the one who eventually learned to take words of criticism (cue the whiplash) and transform them into acknowledgement, and growth. In your case, this may be what you're learning to do, or maybe it's something you're familiar with already. Either way, the refinement of the process on a constant basis is how you continuously improve the structure you work with.

So how do you refine a transformation process?

The inner dialogue is the most ideal-cut, flawless diamond in the rough here. (Or the most logical solution to just about anything you have control over.) Right now, you have a choice to take your life from where it is currently, to the next level, or let it sink. Would it be outrageous to think you won't settle for less than improvement?

(A hint for later on: improvement requires hard, sometimes gruesome work.)

If you could, imagine being faced with a life or death situation. Your life is on the line, and the opportunity to recover or get out of it is within reach, but it's a short road to cracking under pressure. What would your internal dialogue be?

"Should I do this?"

"What if I can't do this?"

"How is my neighbor doing it?"

For many of us, the internal dialogue wouldn't be a conversation, it would be a military drill sergeant giving us the aggressive play-by-play, embedding success into our minds, even with horizon in sight. One moment you look up to check to see if they're still there, and they give you a swift slap to the face and tell you to stay focused.

Step one. Check.

Step two Double check.

Step three. Got it.

And so on.

No voice in between to vocalize "what if's" or "how we failed last time," because failure is a construct to show us where to improve - turn it into feedback, and learn from it, especially when you can't afford the extra time it takes to dwell on it.

No matter the circumstance, it's about being successful in the situation, being the hero, and not letting minor details, however extreme they may look, inhibit how you cross the finish line. You have your definition of success, what it looks like, what it sounds like, hell, maybe it even has a color. The important thing here is that you keep it constant in that it is ever growing alongside you. If your version of success doesn't grow, how you can you expect yourself to?

So, between a life and death situation with an inner drill sergeant and running a business with a constantly growing version of success, what's the difference?

In this moment, right now, what would it take for you be prepared for an internal crisis before it evolves? If you get sidetracked by social media when you still need to bump up your Facebook ads, or write emails to prospects, what is your response? Even though you've been at it for hours, and still haven't gotten to where you want to be, do you scroll for a few hours, or do you discipline yourself until it's done? What is your inner dialogue telling you, and how are you responding?

What does it mean, and what is your definition of "self-discipline," versus what it means to release tension in order to refresh and start anew?

In my practice I deal with a lot of definitions. From defining success to defining loss and what makes it so unbearable. As a Life Coach who focuses primarily on Personal Growth, the tenacity I need to show my clients has to be, bar none, an example they would show their kids. Being a superhero in front of my clients is one page and needing to be my own personal hero is the rest of the book. When something is on a to-do list it has nothing to do with whether or not I want to do it. As of now, it feels great to have priorities and things to work on, but the road to get there was filled with inner talk resembling my old overweight self on the couch in 9th grade eating mashed potatoes because they resembled how I felt. (Not a good look.)

Being resourceful in business is the same as being physically resourceful in life. Did you ever use a step stool growing up? Have you ever used superglue on a cut? Have you ever substituted an ingredient in a recipe and had it still taste to standard? Well congratulations, you've made it past phase one of being resourceful, and like any talent, you now have the opportunity to hone it.

My resourcefulness didn't come from questioning my tactics or believing criticism when it was regurgitated in my lap. Instead it has always been an opportunity to observe my performance, progress, and my ability to be open to constructive feedback. (Even when I saw it as a failure.)

In the time of crisis, it has been a true test of will power and an example of how my inner dialogue reflects my external claim to fame. There is no truer moment than living the reality you continue to *consciously manifest. Going from full-time machinist with a healthy paycheck and part time clients to self-disciplining myself about a marketing plan in order to get one or two new clients this week for the monthly bills was a transition I had never really prepared myself for, but it turns out I became quite good at it when I needed to be.

I told myself when it was appropriate to be dedicated, and when it was rejuvenating to laugh at even the smallest things. What it comes down to is this: whatever you want is up to you to get. Whatever you need to learn in order to obtain it is also yours for the taking, but definitely more important than the goal. What you may yet understand is, if you aren't ready, you simply won't find the resources.

If you need to be patient, but the results you're looking for are instantaneous, you have something to learn. If you're struggling with self-improvement to better your business, or even in general, find out why. Remember the times you accomplished what you thought you couldn't and prove to yourself why it doesn't have to be a one-time act of luck, but rather a glimpse into a small percentage of your capacity to succeed.

Your code to crack is your inner dialogue, but listening to the pronunciation, the inflection, when it's spoken and why, is the science you need to master. Regardless of whether you want to listen or not, you're being spoken to. Your mission, if you're willing to be the best you can be, is to master your own language of internal language and external action. If you believe you can, if you have a big enough goal attached to the desire to fulfill it, you will. I know you've heard this message before, but in a time of crisis, it's either spoken louder than ever, or executed by panic.

If you've picked this book, you already know what path you're on. If you've read this chapter, you've already made a commitment to this path. If you read to the end, not skipping pages, you've fired up your dedication to a point that the momentum will take you to the end, if you let it.

(Let it.)

Become the listener, fluent in your own language.

Let it direct you, the navigator in unknown territories.

Let it teach you and become a teacher to people who are two steps back.

Let it speak for your tenacity, your drive, and your patience for the process.

Become Limitless by showing the rest of the world how to utilize your voice in a way that lets your success speak for itself.

The next time you think it's "too much" remember a time when you thought the same thing, but still surpassed your own limits. Whatever it is that makes you question yourself is there to test you. "Do I really need to send this email today?" Means: "Am I willing get over the procrastination to honor myself and my business?" The coding is simple, and learning it is simple. Even following through is simple. Choose to make it that way.

Now I have some important questions for you: How do you plan to show the world what you're capable of? How do you plan to show the people who look up to you what it means to have tenacity and drive even in the darkest and most confusing moments? (Confusion, after all, simply means you're learning something new.) How do you plan to show yourself that any and all obstacles are obsolete in comparison to what your potential can create?

Now, you could say I went from "lost cause" machinist to Life Coach in a matter of resourceful steps. Yes, I had a whole array of things I needed to prove, but more so, I wanted to be free, to be fulfilled, and to have a successful relationship with myself. (One day I will write a book dedicated to my ambition to help my tribal lands in my philanthropist agenda, but one step along the path at a time.)

I funded my business for some years through machining and hard labor before walking out on my own. That's a story anyone can read. The idea of a pandemic happening the moment I began to learn to fly on my own is almost a complete outline of how my luck fluctuated throughout my entire life, and to be honest, it's gotten to the point where it's become an adventure rather than a setback every time I encounter it. I, for one, enjoy the journey to the top of the mountain. One filled with blisters and uphill pains in my shins, just so looking back at the top of it feels that much rewarding.

A shred of optimism for the young ones - even in fairytales the ending is never an ending. It is a stepping-stone to another learning experience, and whether we want to mold them into happy explorations or not is up to us, and what we tell ourselves. Therefore, I would have to declare, especially in the entrepreneur world, this an endless adventure, one filled and speckled with flourishing continuations.

Thanks for sticking with it,

Kendra

***

To contact Kendra:

kendra.llct@gmail.com

Herbert Lang

An active speaker, entrepreneur, motivator, and author, Herb "Flight Time" Lang is an 18-year former player and coach with the World-Famous Harlem Globetrotters. He is originally from Brinkley, Arkansas, where, as a former All-State Standout athlete, he graduated at the top of his class while serving as senior class president. Herb later obtained a degree in Health and Physical Education from Centenary College of Louisiana in Shreveport. During his tenure there, he led the Trans-America Athletic Conference in scoring and won the National Association of Basketball Coaches Slam Dunk Contest.

Throughout his travels, to nearly 90 countries while entertaining as "Flight Time," some of Herb's most memorable moments include meeting Pope Francis, President Obama, and appearing on numerous national television commercials and reality TV shows—most notably CBS's "The Amazing Race." He currently resides in Sacramento, California, where he is the proud father of two, Nicholas and Reya Lang, and continues to make a difference through kindness and his life experiences, which he believes are the keys to maximizing what we get out of living. He is a true believer that we are all rich with love and kindness.

The Kindness Bridge to Wealth

By Herbert Lang

In May of 2017, my dream job came to an end. For 18 years, I was fortunate and blessed to have traveled the world, putting smiles on the faces of hundreds of thousands of fans covering nearly 90 countries worldwide as "Flight Time" of the Harlem Globetrotters! The most famous sports team in the world, "The World-Famous Harlem Globetrotters," gave me the honor of holding a spot in their organization for nearly 20 years! The knowledge I gathered before and during these amazing times are all experiences that helped direct my journey.

In May of 2019, I released my first book, "Projects, Popes, and Presidents." Since I already wrote one book you can reference, I have decided to pick up here on happenings since my Globetrotting days halted in May of 2017. Ready? Let's take flight!

The Golden Rule says to treat others as you want to be treated. My Golden Rule is to "try treating others even better than you can expect to be treated." My thoughts are that we should all try this pattern of behavior regularly. In this life, like most, I have not lived without moments that occasionally seemed to be setbacks. I have not been perfect, as others have not always treated me the way I think I deserve or deserved at times; that only makes me human. These imperfections make us all human. For those whom I have wronged, I try to make amends, and I hope seeking of forgiveness always works both ways, which leads me to always being thankful.

The 48 hours after my dream job came to an end were possibly some of the most crucial hours of my life! During those two days, I had to make some life-altering decisions that continue to lead me to my ultimate destiny of kindness and a better world for all. I learned to always be thankful for what others give me; that does not always mean monetary things. In 48 hours, I can say without any doubt that every emotion I have in my body was affected. Through it all, I knew the most important thing I had to do for myself was to give thanks.

I needed to go and recognize the people who contributed to giving me 18 years of life experiences I may never have known.

Within that two-day span, I decided I needed to thank as many people as possible for helping me. I wrote several letters doing just that, as I have learned over recent years that writing is an amazing way to let go and often enables us to move forward from things that may be mentally and emotionally holding us back, keeping us from advancing to the next levels of our journey. My next move forward would be to decide where I would live, post Globetrotting, as I had spent the past 23 years in Shreveport-Bossier City, Louisiana, where I graduated from Centenary College as a student-athlete in the late '90s. That part of the world would always be home to me, but I had ultimately decided to move to California, a move I had to make quickly as my apartment lease was coming up for renewal late that July.

On August 1, 2017, I spent my 41st birthday driving cross-country to my new city of residence in Sacramento, California. The move to California was, of course, to the displeasure of many—some I consider close to me. Still, I knew to fulfill my destiny, I had to relocate for a clear path of thinking and creating. There comes a time in life when we get to decide what's best for us and not what others think best may be. I knew I needed a new space and location to put into action things I had been subconsciously creating in my brain for many years while traveling the world and meeting many amazing people.

California was just as beautiful as I remembered from all the other times before. Upon my arrival, I was lucky to not need immediate work. My money situation had not become an issue, thanks to some level-headed negotiations that bought me some time to reboot and begin to put my creative juices into motion. One of the first things I did within a few weeks of arriving was to apply for a ridesharing job with both Uber and Lyft, ultimately working part-time as a Lyft driver, an activity I occasionally enjoy sparingly still today. Ridesharing was and still is one of the most humbling experiences of my life. It gave me the ability to converse with others and gradually put my complaints into perspective. During my 18 years of traveling and the emergence of texting, through rideshare driving, I realized I had lost the ability to engage in the simple act of conversation, something I have since regained.

Rideshare driving also helped me to realize that some of the issues I had daily been complaining about are quite minimal and unimportant. I began to quickly understand how selfish I had become in some of my ways and thinking. I will forever be grateful for my experiences with many of the riders whose stories helped me get through.

With that said, the move to California—like life—was not as smooth as one might have hoped but was undoubtedly worth doing. Within five months of relocating, I was in another situation where I needed to decide rather quickly. I came to California, giving myself a year to settle in and decide if this was the place I was supposed to be. While searching and questioning myself about the whole purpose of my move, the Universe sent me a sign in the form of my new partner in life, Elena—a loving person who also holds attributes of being self-driven, self-motivated, and unafraid to go for "unrealistic dreams."

In February of 2018, after being in Sacramento nearly six months, I began to write my first book, "Projects, Popes, and Presidents." The motivation from Elena helped me complete it in about three months, finally taking the necessary action steps of putting my thoughts and experiences to paper. There were many learning experiences, even within just the first six months. At that time, I signed with an agency to promote and help me transition into the next phase of life post-basketball. It's amazing what you can learn today from Google and YouTube because I was able to develop two treatments for TV show concepts I created on my own through research and self-teaching on how to create television production treatments.

These months also led up to Elena and me taking a three-week trip to Europe in the summer of 2018 with family. This trip opened my eyes to what was truly possible in life. We spent time in Paris, Nice, Monte Carlo, Ibiza, and Barcelona. For the first time, I traveled at a slower pace than I had become accustomed to. It was a pace I had not known during my wonderful time with the Harlem Globetrotters as well as my three seasons of traveling the world on CBS's "The Amazing Race!" This time I had a chance to reflect and see how people lived.

While on this trip, I noticed people were happy and carefree. I remember seeing all the fancy cars and yachts, as well as famous hotels and casinos! This trip made me realize anything was and is possible; this trip showed me that I could do anything in this world I wanted to do. These were no longer just words; I decided to think and create more freely! By no means did I consider myself the smartest person in the world; the Universe simply created people who bring my thoughts and ideas to life. It has created things and people to bring your creations to life as well. We all get to be of service to one another.

Traveling through Europe, I began to realize that everything I needed to attain all the things I wanted, life had already presented to me. The wealth of knowledge I had achieved in my travels, as well as the relationships and connections I'd made along the way, began to re-appear in my thoughts. I began to think about my family, friends, colleagues, and the many incredible, diverse people I had met over my nearly 90 countries visited. I have had many extraordinary experiences up to this point in my life is what I realized. Now it was time to honestly figure out how to put my ideas into motion and make them a reality. After all those thoughts and upon returning from Europe, I decided it was time to find work.

I chose Life Insurance, an area of expertise my uncle Mike Curry of Memphis, Tennessee, recommended highly based on his 40 plus years in the business. After prepping for and passing the California Health and Life Insurance Exam, I took a job with American Income Life Insurance Company. I learned much during my time there! For instance, how to let the "no's" roll off my shoulders and to keep positive thoughts going into every opportunity because you never know if that next call or door knock will be the opportunity to provide some kind of security in the lives of the families on the receiving end of your presentation. I would be lying if I said it was easy. The *no's* hurt very much in the beginning. As a former athlete,

I had become accustomed to hearing, "Yes! Yes! Yes!" This experience was exactly what I needed to help me remember and appreciate hard work—along with the rewards that come along with hard work and perseverance.

Something I learned as a Globetrotter is that sometimes we get to entertain ourselves. I can remember making my first phone calls to potential clients. Most of the people were kind and willing to listen, but the ones who didn't want to talk would quickly let it be known! I remember vividly many times making calls only to get hung up on immediately or mid-conversation. I decided to have a little fun with it and called some of those who would hang up unexpectantly and say, "Oh, my goodness! I'm sorry. I have been having a bad connection all day. As I was saying before my phone disconnected us…" Surprisingly, some people would essentially hear me out after this reason, although *they'd* hung up on me. *Ha!*

Another thing I learned came from my manager, Bruce Alford, while working in the Insurance Industry. The lesson came in a simple question his father asked about his dreams. Bruce's father asked, "Son, have you given up on your dreams or forgotten about them?" This comment and shared moment pushed me even more forward in realizing that even in my 40's, I get to dream the same way I did as a kid! Some of the dreams may not be as realistic as the dreams from my childhood due to Father Time, but I get to keep dreaming. We all get to keep dreaming and setting goals! I get to show my kids and those kids who never saw me as "Flight Time" that Herb is more than the old athlete they may hear stories about. I have been blessed to experience many remarkable things in my life. I also get to do even more astonishing things and show people from all walks of life that like in my life, anything is and will be possible if we move into the space of possibility and never allow ourselves to become stuck in a tradition that doesn't work or making circles with no plans of advancing.

After six months in the insurance business, I decided it was time for me to move forward with the next phase of life. Toward the end of my time in the industry, Elena presented me with the next opportunity that would significantly shift my life and help me realize there is always room to grow! For me, this opportunity came upon agreeing to attend and complete leadership training! From March through June of 2019, I would spend three months of learning and growing with Heart Core Leadership (HCL) in San Diego, California. During those months, I was fortunate to be surrounded by people who helped me to see possibilities within myself that I now know are limitless. Heart Core made Zoom video conferencing cool before Zoom recently became super cool to me and the rest of the world!

While training and since my life has shifted dramatically, this is when I realized I had already crossed "The Kindness Bridge to Wealth." I was now able to reflect on my life and appreciate that I had already experienced much of what I wanted. I began to understand how important it is to **include others** in my vision and my dreams. One of the most valuable lessons I learned is the extreme importance of putting thoughts and ideas into action. I have since created more opportunities to be part of many other awesome events, speak to thousands of children, and comprehend what I get to create as well as help make the world a better place.

In this season, I have been privileged to connect with many wonderful people. During this dreadful pandemic of 2020, we all get to grow and learn. I used almost every tool possible to connect with the world and build my brand while spreading hope and kindness at the same time. For my daughter, we connected on Tic Toc while my son and I connected on Xbox. I was able to make these connections, at the same time, thinking of marketing ideas for these same platforms. It had been 20 years since I seriously played video games.

As adults, we forget what it was like to be kids. We all get to remember! We also get to smarten up and be open to this awesome, ever-changing world. There is much peace, freedom, and wealth in this way of thinking. These memories and experiences are all part of our "bridge." Regarding "The Bridge to Wealth," or anything you envision, don't be afraid to re-visit with the possibility of discovering something you may have glanced over along the journey. Don't be scared to engage in the ever-rapid evolving world we get to live in. Statistics say that much of the world participates in some form of social media, which is fine. I just say to everyone, "Be open and don't be afraid to explore."

Since becoming an entrepreneur, I also realized that I get to bet on me! I became visible and active on all the major platforms of social media: Facebook, Instagram, Twitter, Tic Toc, and LinkedIn. I encourage all entrepreneurs and big dreamers to use these platforms in the best ways you can for your businesses. Most recently, my investment in obtaining a professional LinkedIn profile has given me access to more doors than I could have imagined! I get to go all-in on me and trust that the Universe is in alignment with the understanding that betting on me means betting on you and the rest of the world!

I challenge those who spend hundreds of dollars at bars, on cars, shoes, jewelry, homes, and other material things to also spend money on professional business profiles and professional development tools that allow us to grow outside the norm. Spend a little of that shoe money on promoting something you have created and strongly believe in! Don't be afraid to bet on yourself! The world gets to win! We all get to win! Let's go! Our Bridges got us here and will continue helping us along the way.

One of the smartest things I was able to do during my traveling days was to save for my future. Well, my future is today! Your future is today! As a kid, I fell in love with sports, and sports took me around the world. The world showed me the power of kindness. The connections (friends) along the way I've made have granted me numerous timely business ventures and continue to do so. Everything I am and have involved myself in is a result of the bridges crossed and kindness given and received along the way. I chose an education degree because of the bridge that was my high school basketball coach! I chose to get into TV post basketball because of my cameos on numerous television shows! I chose to form my own sports brand, Swag Ball, because of the "bridge" that is the Harlem Globetrotters!

In all those instances, I hope you can see the importance of the Bridges (Connections). The patience and kindness others have instilled in me were given freely along the way, and these are the attributes I'm grateful are free. These things cost us nothing. *"Kindness is free!"* Give it away! Give, give, give, and enjoy the feeling that comes over you, knowing you have potentially given joy to another individual. We are all already rich with our natural God-given qualities. Use them freely and let these ways guide you to your wildest dreams.

One more thing, while on your journey, do not succumb to the naysayers! Many people ask me about my process of book-writing, which—for me again—was research on popular search engines like Google and YouTube. The actual act of taking time to apply what you learn is what many aspiring writers struggle with in getting started. Writing is becoming easier in this new age of technology because technology allows us to see the world in ways many of us could have never imagined unless, like myself, you had traveled to many of these places. Still, it's your journey! Don't be afraid to take chances. Explore the possibilities this game of life has for you. Play hard, play fair, and play all out! Your "kindness bridge" to the life you dream of is up to you! Go for it!

***

To contact Herb:

Website: www.herblang.com,

LinkedIn: www.linkedin.com/in/themotivationalspeaker

Facebook: (www.facebook.com/datrotter4

Twitter: @datrotter4

Joy Ross

Joy is an Author, Visual Artist, Feng Shui Designer, Educator and Speaker, Visionary, Aromatherapist, Aesthetician, and Reiki Master.

With thirty-five years in the service industry developing strong relationships with clients and students alike, Joy has always had a love of sharing her passions! She brings her unwavering commitment to personal development and a desire to embrace all the joy and deliciousness of life to everything she does! She facilitates learning that deepens self-understanding, knowledge and joy! She encourages her students and clients to actualize their dreams through various modalities and with tools that inspire clarity and alignment through joy.

She is currently penning her first book, *Indelible Vision*, the inspiring story of her father, Michael Tyrrell's remarkable life following a devastating mining accident at age 23, that left him near death, totally blind and an amputee, yet moving forward fearlessly to create a life of self-mastery!

The Pursuit of Excellence

By Joy Ross

I became an entrepreneur because as far back as I can remember, I have always believed that **anything is possible!!!** I learnt this at a young age as I watched my hero, my Father, navigate the world. That may not sound like anything special but, long before I was born, events unfolded that would significantly impact my Father and his then fiancée, my Mother, and eventually myself and my younger Sister.

In August of 1960 when my Father, Michael Tyrrell, was just 23 years old, he miraculously survived a devastating mining accident in Cold Stream Mine, about 80 miles north of Thunder Bay, Ontario, Canada. It may have seemed just like any other regular workday, but it was truly a day like no other. It was that fateful day that changed Michael's life, and subsequently our lives forever! Working the stope just below the 350 ft. level, a series of 17 holes were drilled 12 ft. into the rock face and were then loaded and connected. Ten sticks of dynamite were placed in the next hole and being tamped, when all 20 sticks of dynamite exploded prematurely in Michael's face! The insurmountable devastation of that accident left him clinging to life, and with multiple compound fractures, including facial bone and skull fractures, multiple lacerations to the skull, nose and mouth, and muscle injury to the left thigh. Further, extensive damage to his left forearm, wrist and fingers resulting in amputation of the left arm, wrist and hand below the elbow. Chunks of ore deeply embedded in his left leg muscles, rendered the leg paralysed. Believing the darkness engulfing him after the blast was due to an electrical breakdown caused by the explosion, he was unaware that the most dreadful of his injuries was to his eyes. He was completely blinded. Both eyes were destroyed in the blast.

The ensuing months were filled with countless plastic surgeries to repair damage done to his face in the explosion. Extensive dental work was required. Rehabilitation was needed to strengthen his left arm stump in order to be fitted with an artificial arm. The left leg gradually regained its mobility and strength. Learning to walk without sight, is one of the initial obstacles posed by blindness, and to be good at it requires diligence and many hours of practice. The development of manual dexterity is also vital and the foundation for all future manual accomplishments, therefore this training is rigorous and ongoing. Then there was the monumental task of learning to read, write and type braille with one hand.

In July of 1961 my parents, Diane and Michael were married. Following the wedding they sailed to Dublin, Ireland to honeymoon and reunite with Michael's family. Michael had emigrated from Ireland in 1957. In the spring of 1962, I was born in Dublin. During their extended stay in Ireland, it became apparent that there was little opportunity for employment for someone with my father's disabilities. So, they looked to Canada for a more promising future and sailed back late in 1962.

It became apparent that in order to move forward my Father would need a high school education so in the fall of 1963 Michael entered the Ontario School for the Blind. He was 27 years old, married, and a father of one, and in the 9th grade! Back home in Ireland, he left school at age 14 to work as a telegram delivery boy. Late in 1964, when Michael was in grade 10 our family welcomed my Sister.

Many more years of school followed, as Michael finished high school and attended university. I watched my Father walk to university by himself and with only a white cane to navigate his way there and to classes around campus. I observed him for hours, listening to his lessons and textbooks that had been recorded on tape. He composed and transcribed all his study notes in braille. In 1971 he graduated university with an Honors Bachelor's Degree in Sociology and Psychology from Wilfrid Laurier University, Waterloo, Ontario, Canada. After graduating he was hired as a case worker for the local chapter of Big Brothers, where he continued to work for over 30 years until his retirement.

Daily, I watched my Father accomplish what seem like simple tasks. Buttoning his shirt, tying his tie, tying his shoelaces, (no Velcro in those days!) and zipping up his jacket were all part of his regular morning routine. All of these seemingly trivial, ordinary tasks were accomplished without sight and with the only one hand. He did all this in a timely fashion and without complaint. In fact, he did it with gratitude and joy in his heart, and all before he left for work each morning! It was clear to anyone who encountered Michael that he lived his life with gratitude and joy, and anyone who knew my Father would agree that he had a beautiful love affair with life! In every moment he was grateful simply to be alive!

Michael's pursuit of excellence did not stop with those achievements! Over the years he volunteered in the community he loved, acting as a counsellor for organizations such as K-W Kops Cadet Group, Ignatius College and Loyola House, and serving as Chairman of the CNIB Advisory Board, and Chairman of St. Michael's Community Workers Council to name a few. He was a regular blood donor for the rest of his life following the accident.

At age 50 my Father started running and this provided him with another set of challenges as he developed new skills. He became an Executive Member of the Ontario Blind Sports Association and competed at the Masters level. He honed his training to include javelin, discus and shot put in addition to running 100 metres, 200 metres, 400 metres, 800 metres and 1500 metres races. Always aiming to improve on his personal best times, he continued to excel and break many Canadian Records, both at the Provincial and National levels, in all events!

> *"In sport, as in life in general, the pursuit of excellence needs to be a constant goal."*
>
> - Michael Tyrrell

Michael's life exemplified this philosophy. First and foremost, came the needs of his family. He was a doting father and an amazing mentor to both my Sister and I, and to countless others. He was a touchstone for many and was always available with a listening ear. His advice was rooted in sensibility and deep faith. He impacted scores of lives in his personal and professional life. He walked his talk! His life was one of true self-mastery!

When you are struggling and in your victimology, I encourage you to pause and attempt to tie your shoes with one hand. Better yet, go and do it right now! Yes, I mean now! How long until you are ready to give up? Now close your eyes and try again! Imagine the patience and perseverance and courage required if these were your circumstances for the rest of your life! Would you want to roll over and die, or would you accept what is, and get about the business of embracing the truth, that you are bigger and better than your circumstances? Would you choose to move forward fearlessly, with determination and a belief that where there is a will, there is a way? Or would you prefer folding yourself into a fetal position, angry and bitter about your lot in life? Would you be engulfed by your grief and pain, or would you choose to rise, and to rise again each day? Would you trust that everything is given to us out of love and for our highest good? Would you face each day with gratitude and see each experience as love expressing itself to you through all the wonderful gifts of the Universe, regardless of whether you deem them good or bad?

The truth that we hold dear is what our lives come to be made of. What we hold as "truth" quickly becomes manifest in our lives. Life mirrors thought and ideas motivate us to action. Since thoughts create and drive our actions, one can only imagine how different Michael Tyrrell's story could have read had he not believed in a truth that kept him buoyant as he faced and scaled so very many obstacles!

My Mother taught me about having faith in something greater. Her unwavering faith in God and herself, kept her focused on the outcome of marriage that their engagement signified months before the circumstances radically changed, with Michael's mining accident. My parents were the ideal example of what it means to be steadfast and to never give up! My Father with his unfailing gratitude and determination, and my Mother with her unwavering commitment as his caregiver. Together, they were a force to be reckoned with!

Physics teaches that everything is energy and what we choose to focus on expands. Where our intention goes, energy flows, and momentum builds! Intention creates your reality consciously and with reverence. By stating your intention as you work through the many moving parts of your day, you bring a clarity of focus to everything you do. Adjust your intention each time you change your activity. Keep your thoughts pinpointed on your intention and add to it; "With gratitude, this, or something better!", to reinforce your potential willingness to be open to the best possible outcome! Intention brings mindfulness and presence to your experiences. Move with intention, think with intention, love with intention, act with intention and you will raise your vibration!

Cultivate a sacred space inside yourself, wherein lies the light of your awareness. Trust in your ability to shine this light on your intuition. Regularly tuning into your intuition helps you get to know it, trust it and to assuredly follow its guidance. Trusting your intuition builds confidence in your ability to discern your next right inspired action! Cultivate your intuition daily and nurture your capacity to visualize the outcome (or something better) that you desire. Journaling and meditation are two of the best tools for this. Delegate a space in your home that is peaceful and devoid of distraction and practice connecting to your intuition daily. Sacred space exists where you deem it so, and when prefaced with your intention. Intend to develop a direct connection with your intuition. Clarity comes when you accept what IS, stop asking "why?" and start asking "how?". When you laser-focus on the outcome you desire and do not let the current set of circumstances distract you in any way from that which you endeavor to accomplish, you will develop a clarity of vision. We all have an internal compass. A quiet place inside us that prompts and points us in the right direction. This is the womb of creation where hope and pure potentiality reside. Once connected to this energy, it is easy to spot magic in your life! Synchronicities are Divine gifts and provide guideposts along your path! When you are in this flow it feels like magic! Be aware of your thoughts and take note of the areas of your life where you limit the potential for something greater. Always trust your instincts and never give up!

Have faith in a higher order and be willing to connect, communicate, collaborate, and co-create with Spirit, God, Creator, whatever title resonates for you! Choose to trust in the Creator's ability to always bring you what is best for you! Believe in love and its healing force! Believe in yourself, your abilities, your journey and your willingness to learn, to evolve and to become all that you can be! Conceive of an alternate reality that is remarkably different than the one that lies in front of you. Push your mind beyond what is obvious, and into the realm of pure potentiality. In other words, you can only see miracles when you believe they are possible! Ask yourself, "What have I got to lose by believing in the best possible outcome?"

In joy there is no sorrow! Face each day with an open heart. Michael chose to live in gratitude and with joy. Our family rose above challenges with the wonderful, healing gift of humour. Dad was particularly fond of puns and he used his quick wit to make us laugh daily! Drink in all the beauty, and deliciousness of life! Find the priceless gift of joy wherever you are, regardless of the circumstances. If you can't find joy, create some!

I am living, breathing, walking, talking proof that these tools work! I am certain that if I did not use these tools that are in my "life skills toolbox", I might not be here talking with you today! In February of 2013, and just a few months after my Father's passing, I was vacationing in Florida. In the early morning of the day I was scheduled to fly home to Ontario, Canada, I had to visit the emergency room. Within a few hours I was informed I had a massive cancerous tumor on my right kidney. I would require emergency surgery to remove both the tumor and the kidney. Late that evening I flew home in an air ambulance. I was grateful to be reunited with my family and in our local hospital. I spent the following nine days waiting on diagnostics and to be stable enough to undergo surgery. Those days were some of the most demanding days of my life! They came and went slowly, with the gravity of not knowing if I would live or die, weighing heavily. The burden of uncertainty was indescribable! I quickly realized that if I believed that this diagnosis (circumstances) would kill me, I would most certainly perish! I also knew that if I could conceive, focus on, and believe in the best possible outcome, it would exist in the womb of pure potentiality. Then, and only then, would that reality be a possibility!

I was grateful to have had excellent care in Florida at Cape Canaveral Hospital. I was grateful to have been safely delivered back to my hometown and to be reunited with my family. I was grateful to be in hospital and that I was being well cared for. I appreciated finally knowing what was happening in my body, as I had suffered several years with undiagnosed pain. I appreciated and sent love to everyone and everything that was supporting me on my journey! I found that the singularity of focusing on that which I was grateful for, kept my mind present and peaceful and able to envision the best possible outcome! In my heart I was sincerely grateful for everything, including the diagnosis and even the very unfashionable hospital gown! I connected with my intention to meet each moment with acceptance and gratitude.

I remember the faces of friends and family who very kindly came to visit me, during what might have been my last days. In each interaction I aimed to bring my fearless self! I brought joy, laughter and a light heart so that the dread on their faces would melt away. I asked myself; "If this were to be my last interaction with this person, what do I want her or him to recall?" I thought about my legacy and how I would be remembered. I brought my best self to all my encounters and continued to focus on the potential for a successful outcome! I practiced gratitude and connected with my intention to meet every day with acceptance and appreciation and I lived each of those challenging days with my truth; that although I may have been at my lowest, I could still choose to bring joy to those around me. I accepted what was and I kept the faith that Spirit could deliver more miracles! On February 28, 2013 I underwent a successful surgery to remove my right kidney and the massive Stage IV carcinoma that was .5 mm from the margin of the kidney!

Due to the size of the tumor the surgery could not be performed laparoscopically, thereby lengthening recovery time. I continued to excel in spite of my physical limitations, making small strides daily. I honed my focus and cultivated my clarity of vision for an outcome of vibrant health and wellbeing. I lived and continue to live in gratitude, noting my blessings daily, the greatest of which is to be alive! In gratitude there is no fear, just appreciation! I trust in the ability of my body to know how to heal. I am open and willing to co-create with Spirit!

Abundance comes in many different forms, not just monetary. Mindfully intend to see all the abundance in your life. What you focus on will expand. Align with gratitude and attract more abundance! Bring faith, intention, appreciation, clarity of vision and joy into your life daily, living your truth and walking in beauty! These practices enhance all aspects of life, be it in business, or life in general. They are tools to elevate our vibration, to open our hearts and to assist us in the continuing pursuit of excellence!

I trust that life is a magical journey and Spirit is in the business of creating miracles all around us and in our lives, daily!

In the true entrepreneurial spirit, I continue to believe that...

ANYTHING IS POSSIBLE!

***

To contact Joy:

aligningjoy.com

aligningjoy@gmail.com

facebook.com/Aligningjoy-100820114940268/

instagram.com/alignjoy/

pinterest.com/Aligningjoy

Lauren Brenner

Lauren Brenner has an eclectic background. A Division 1 tennis player to a Wall Street trader, spending eight years on the NYSE, and obtaining five licenses. Lauren then combined her three passions—sports, entertainment, and business—and redefined fitness. She opened the nation's first indoor obstacle/confidence course called "Pure Power Boot Camp," which had three company locations and was licensed to franchise in forty-three states.

Appearing as a weekly fitness contributor on the *Today Show* and on numerous major networks, Lauren received national acclaim and was named "The number 1 entrepreneur making an impact on the nation" by CNN.

Today, Lauren is a motivational speaker working with companies, universities, and schools, employing her innate ability to connect with all audiences. She is recognized as the 'go-to' motivational influencer emphasizing perseverance and resilience for sales forces in the doldrums.

Lauren speaks to students and parents on the dangers of social media and cyberbullying, and her "Bring Back Childhood" movement is gaining momentum. Her podcast, *Empowered with Lauren*, focuses on women leading by example to be role models to young girls and strives to build a society where women stand for women.

Lauren is a work in progress, constantly evolving and fueling her fire. Her family—husband Mikel, daughter Jaxy, cat Layla and dog Eden form the nucleus of her heart.

Fuel Your Fire and Own It

By Lauren Brenner

If it were not for perseverance and resilience, and if I did not have the foundation of the entrepreneurial tools that I am about to impart, I either would have been broken, curled up in a fetal position, or in a padded cell, and I *definitely* would have been bankrupt.

There are two different kinds of people in the world: SPECTATORS and PLAYERS. Spectators are those inert individuals who sit on the sidelines and live vicariously through others' experiences and actions. They are voyeurs, devoid of purpose and fire, and usually feed off the energy and vitality of the player.

Players are active participants who embrace life's highs and lows with GRIT and PASSION. They enjoy a challenge and are, in fact, fueled by it, understanding that success does not come knocking at their door. Players know that they must *create* and *own* it. As an entrepreneur, YOU are the truest definition of a "player."

A genuine player in life breaks through the facades and emerges as the most authentic representative of active engagement and participation in the *real* human experience. As an entrepreneur, YOU are a creator, making an indelible imprint on society by using your imagination and talents.

Much of society functions on perception and often negates reality. Social media is the prime vehicle which perpetuates smoke and mirrors and enshrouds us in illusory versions of the truth, causing us to lose sight of our authenticity. The instant gratification of this medium gives us false present sense impressions of who we are.

The process of becoming an entrepreneur involves a conscious shift—surrendering the vicarious experience (i.e., living *through* or *for* the approval of others) to creating and manifesting *your own reality*. Your internal odyssey, however uncomfortable or intimidating at first, will launch you into self-revelation, an essential element in finding your passion, fueling your fire, and OWNING IT!

The first step is to commit to self-validation. Self-validation is the act of unconditionally embracing who you are—with abandon. At the same time, it involves surrendering extrinsic accolades and criticisms to an internal acceptance of yourself—your thoughts, feelings, emotions, and a recognition of your inherent worth. (Note that self-validation is distinguished from narcissism, which gives you a false sense of superiority, to the negation of your authentic self.)

Instead of being swept up in the hyperbole of "likes" and external validation, you must truly understand what it means to be comfortable in your own skin, regardless of the opinions, thoughts, and judgments of others. The process of endorsing yourself releases you from the unnecessary outside noise that threatens to extinguish your fire. Trust me, when you are at the top of your game, there will be people and events that will threaten to extinguish your fire. Self-validation will be one of the most effective tools in your toolbox to help you weather the obstacles that you inevitably will face as an entrepreneur. Once you block out the chatter and think outside the box—all the while celebrating who you are—you will discover what truly inspires you, and you will continue to fuel what makes you exquisitely *you*.

The personality of an entrepreneur is characterized by intense self-discipline, tenacity, audacity, passion, and risk-taking. Remember, the journey *is* the adventure when you engage in the creative process.

Merely showing up and checking in will not and does not cut it. It is *how* you show up that matters. A vital coping skill that you must acquire is becoming comfortable with being uncomfortable. Step outside your comfort zone and ask yourself, "What helps me to evolve moment by moment, even in the most stressful situations? How do I feel about pressure? What makes me uncomfortable?"

Do it! Get comfortable being uncomfortable! All of us are painfully aware that life is comprised of a series of tragedies and disappointments. The outcome of any given circumstance depends on how you react to negative, seemingly insurmountable obstacles. You are *not* defined by a setback. Instead, you are defined by your ability to dust yourself off and use that setback as fuel. Remember these specific words and repeat them over and over to yourself—your mantra: "PERSEVERANCE and RESILIENCE are paramount in the life of any entrepreneur."

One would think that the following story is fictitious, filled with a nefarious cast of villains. However, this was my reality. I was trapped in a nightmare that lasted for years on end. Having taken all the necessary precautionary steps to protect my entrepreneurial concept and after having spent hundreds of thousands of dollars in legal bills, I then had everything stolen from me. Brace yourself and pour yourself a cocktail. It is one wild ride!

For eight years, I was a Wall Street trader on the floor of the New York Stock Exchange. After 9/11, I was in my third phase of testing with the FBI (I wanted to be part of the anti-terrorist unit, but no one has a choice as to which unit they are assigned.) The truth was, I was intrigued by going through boot camp. I also knew that, at that moment in time, the world had changed forever, and people—especially Americans— wanted to become physically and emotionally stronger. So, I decided to combine my three passions of sports, entertainment, and business and fuel my entrepreneurial fire.

I had been a Division 1 tennis player in college, I also spent time as one of the leads in the longest-running off-Broadway show, *Tony and Tina's Wedding* and, as I mentioned, I had been a Wall Street trader for years. It seemed like the perfect trifecta to launch a new venture. Therefore, I developed the idea of creating the nation's first and only indoor obstacle/confidence course for civilians. To hone my innovation, I visited Fort Knox in Louisville, KY (an over 109,050-acre military base), and I adapted thirteen obstacles that I scaled down and built to simulate an indoor military training facility. I found a 6,500 square-foot loft in Chelsea to call home. From then on, fitness was redefined. Pure Power Boot Camp ("PPBC") was born.

Strapped for cash, I had to be a one-woman operation, painting ninety-five percent of the place myself and sleeping on the floor. I had to prove to myself and to all the naysayers out there that I was going to make my vision come to fruition.

Failure was not an option.

Literally stepping outside my comfort zone, I stood on the corner on Fifth Avenue in a camouflage bikini and military fatigues. On a snowy December day, in thirty-eight-degree temperatures, I was wielding a blow horn, blowing a whistle, and screaming at the top of my lungs like a lunatic, while handing out flyers to people passing by. Can you imagine? What a sight. One could have questioned my sanity, but never my passion.

My *insanity* actually paid off. Three weeks into the opening, Monica Novotny, a reporter for MSNBC's *Countdown with Keith Olbermann*, walked in with a flyer in hand and took a class. She returned with a crew, and BAM! Pure Power Boot Camp became *Countdown's* featured number one story. I then retained one of the leading intellectual property firms in the country to register and protect my proprietary information.

Four months into operation, I received incessant calls from a former Army officer in Michigan who purportedly had venture capitalists' backing and was obsessed with demonstrating his vision, in the hope of expanding his brand. Impressed by his persistence, I flew to Michigan, where a series of events occurred that film writers never could even attempt to conjure. In the midst of the mayhem, I shattered my tibia, fibula, and talus in my right ankle and ruptured all the ligaments in my leg. My foot turned black, and I lost the blood supply to that area.

When I returned to NY, the doctors told me that I was in danger of an amputation! (This was one of those events that threatened to extinguish my fire.)

During my time in the hospital, my clients showed unflagging love, belief, and support for me and PPBC. They all signed up for three to six months in advance so that I would stay afloat and not lose revenue. (I still get tears in my eyes when I recall their devotion.) I underwent major reconstructive surgery and had a plate and nine pins placed inside.

Within two weeks of surgery and in tremendous pain, the doors were back open, and I returned to work, teaching on crutches for seven months. For four of those months, I could not weight bear at all. I underwent physical therapy four days a week for three hours a day and worked tirelessly to stave off a limp and regain my athletic prowess. I had all my calls from PPBC forwarded to my cell, and I continued to do all my PR and increase my sales. Talk about using a setback as fuel! I was tougher, wiser, and more resilient. PPBC grew exponentially, and I added more and more classes. At this point, it was time to hire a full staff.

I wanted authenticity, so I reached out to the marine reserve base in Garden City, NY. I decided to hire a staff exclusively comprised of former marines who were having a hard time reintegrating into society. I wanted them to have a career, not just a job. The difficult part was to reprogram their thinking. They were accustomed to the marine corps philosophy, which is to break you down and then rebuild you. PPBC's philosophy was the complete antithesis. Everything was done from the standpoint of inspiring and empowering only through positive reinforcement. I personally trained all of them on the curriculum and taught them how to work with civilians of all shapes and sizes. I became particularly close to Ruben, a kid with barely a high school education, who had previously earned a meager 24k annual salary. He became like a brother to me, and I even paid for his wedding. Over time, I came to trust him so completely that I hired his roommate, Alex (ignoring my intuitive red flags).

Two weeks after getting off crutches, NBC called and asked me to do a fitness segment, which landed me as their paid fitness expert on the *Today Show*, appearing weekly. Shortly thereafter, CNN's Anderson Cooper named me the number one entrepreneur making an impact on the nation. During the next four years, I crushed it! I was the host of a fitness series on the Discovery network and appeared in over twenty-six reality television shows as a fitness guru. My image was displayed everywhere on New York City buses and in taxicabs. I was a financial rock star—printing cash. I proceeded to obtain licenses to franchise in forty-three states. *USA Today* named PPBC the premier franchise to buy. I had over two hundred twenty-six inquiries to purchase a franchise, and I had three company locations— in Jericho, Fort Lauderdale, and Las Vegas— scheduled to open within three months apart.

Prior to the Jericho location's opening, I wanted to hire more staff, but Ruben and Alex insisted on having more hours to increase their earnings. Ruben also told me that one of my instructors was not performing his job well, and because I trusted him so much, I listened to him and fired the guy. At the same time, I offered Ruben a forty-nine percent partnership in the location. To my surprise, he declined, stating that he was in the middle of a contentious divorce and did not want to involve me in any "trouble." Never in my wildest dreams or my worst nightmare could I have envisioned what lay ahead.

Simply put, SHIT hit the fan. Five weeks after the opening of the Jericho location, my assistant went to the front desk computer, intending to open a Hotmail account. By happenstance, she found two hundred fifty-four emails, saved in "favorites," revealing a criminal conspiracy to steal my business. Over the course of seven months, the conspirators, none other than Alex and Ruben (my "brother"), had sinister, clandestine communications with their secret girlfriends, Nancy and Jennifer, both of whom were current clients of mine for almost four years. As part of their plan, all four conspirators hid their romantic connections from my clients and me. Behind my back, they were spreading rumors and poisoning clients against me, while strategizing their treacherous plot to steal everything that I had worked so hard to achieve.

In the emails, Alex and Ruben talked about how they broke into my office and physically stole their noncompete agreements, my business plan, start-up and operations manuals, and the first two chapters of the self-help book that I was writing. They stole and claimed the title as the name of their competing business and downloaded 1,767 clients' personal information off my computer.

PPBC, my brainchild, had fallen prey to the most insidious case of moral turpitude imaginable. Alex's secret girlfriend, Jennifer, who had been part of a celebrity chef's executive team, financed the scheme, dubbing herself "Miss Conversion." Jennifer stated, in several emails, that her primary objective in architecting this plan was to become Alex's wife. A graduate of Wharton Business School, Jennifer, and the others capitalized on her 'education' for the malicious purpose of converting my proprietary information as theirs and circumventing the noncompete clauses. The conspirators destroyed my equipment and left the place in shambles.

When I drove in from Jericho to face the devastation and confront Ruben by phone, his reply was, "I always told you that you were too nice and too trusting." No joke! Those were his *exact* words, and I had a few choice words of my own for him.

I immediately went into damage control and salvation mode to save my entire business. I canceled my franchise plan, as I could not, in good conscience, sell franchises while my business was under attack. I also canceled the two other leases that I had previously scheduled to open.

In an instant, everything I worked for and all my investments—especially my blood and sweat—were about to slip through my fingers.

I blocked out the chatter and all the outside noise that bombarded me and tapped into the entrepreneurial fire that burned inside my gut. If not for self-validation and knowing who I was and what I was made of, I would have crumbled. Instead, I sprang into action.

I reached out to the New York District Attorney's office and was initially informed that they would press criminal charges against Ruben and Alex. A few days later, however, the assistant district attorney called to tell me that she was going on maternity leave and the DA's office was short-staffed. Therefore, she stated, "Because you are high-profile and in the media, you must have the financial means to pay out of pocket, bring suit in civil court, and receive a verdict within two years."

Shocked and infuriated, I hired a civil attorney who attached the two hundred fifty-four emails to a temporary restraining order. In response, the thugs counterclaimed, and the sideshow began. The theft of my business and all my proprietary information was placed on hold, and the case focused on a technicality. Although the felonious emails were on my computer, they were stored on a Hotmail server (not a PPBC server), and unbelievably, there were allegations of unlawful access. This fiasco lasted for over a year, which gave the criminals the opportunity to open their business with my clientele and all my proprietary documents.

I was bleeding cash, dealing with lawyers for hours a day, trying to save my flagship location in NYC, and hiring new staff, all while owning and running my second location in Jericho. On a regular basis, I was putting out fires that the defendants ignited in posts on many different media sites and being comfortable in my own skin became a critical tool for self-preservation.

Although I had a loaded gun — conclusive evidentiary proof of the defendants' guilt—I could not use the emails as ammunition to restore my reputation because they were part of the legal proceedings. During the entire time, the criminals were claiming everything as their mastermind—fourteen blocks away from me! They created *nothing*. They were not entrepreneurs; they were not players; they were not even spectators. They were just thieves. Their talent was their ability to steal. It was mind-blowing— totally surreal!

Do you think that at that point, I wanted to crawl up into my bed and just cry? One hundred percent, but I would *never* give the vermin that victory—*not ever!* I was determined to prove that I would never back down or allow the circumstances to break me. Yes, without a doubt I was uncomfortable, but I dug down deep, dusted myself off, and guess what? I THRIVE when I am uncomfortable. GAME ON!

Although I was fighting for everything I had, I continued to fuel my fire. I re-entered the media, secured a patent on a new fitness product, and sold out three times on QVC. I also launched fitness DVDs and a fitness app. Despite the tremendous obstacles, the outside chatter, and the pain, I was still me— the player, the entrepreneur—still in the game, still fueling my fire, still creating.

Notwithstanding incidents of extortion and an attorney's disbarment, I endured three and a half years of legal wrangling before finally proceeding to trial. Although I was deeply gratified by the defendants' humiliation on the stand, and I received vindication through a finding of their guilt, my compensatory damages award was merely a fraction of the $1.59 million that I had spent in legal fees. At the eleventh hour, in a final twist of fate, I was blindsided by the fact that my intellectual property attorney filed my registrations incorrectly and drafted my nondisclosure agreement improperly. You could not make this up!

Keeping true to myself and standing up for who I am, I brought suit against my attorneys. A decade later, I finally received a seven-figure settlement.

As to the fate of the malicious dirtbags: Jennifer and Alex did get married and soon divorced as a result of Alex's cheating, while Ruben and Alex's partnership dissolved due to "irreconcilable differences." All I can say on that is, "Karma is a real BITCH...."

Life is a proliferation of energy that breeds more energy. Positive and negative energy reproduce themselves. Crises happen, and your success will be tested repeatedly. As an entrepreneur, you must constantly evolve, find new ways to fuel your power, stay present, hungry, and remain in the game. When you encounter that brick wall—or parasitic thieves, as I did—remember that *true success is defined by you, the player—the active participant in life—the entrepreneur—who embodies perseverance and resilience and never allows anyone or anything to steal your fire!*

***

To contact Lauren

Phone: 917-463-6599

Email: Lauren@EmpoweredwithLauren.com

Website: https://empoweredwithlauren.com/

Podcast: https://empoweredwithlauren.com/podcasts/

LinkedIn: https://www.linkedin.com/in/lauren-brenner-99880832/

Facebook: https://www.facebook.com/lauren.empowered

Instagram: https://www.instagram.com/empoweredwithlauren/

YouTube: https://www.youtube.com/channel/UCogqal7dF9yckciJj1LW-Rg

Twitter: https://twitter.com/laurenempowered

Kelly O'Keefe Voorhees

Kelly Voorhees is a professional life coach with Coach Forward LLC®. She has a Master's of Science in Public Health, is an Associate Certified Coach with the International Coach Federation (ICF), and is a Certified Fearless Living Coach and Trainer. She has coached with the Regional Institute of Health and Environmental Leadership since 2008 and continues to provide peer coaching with this organization. Kelly worked in public health for the State of Colorado for over 30 years until 2017, when she became a full-time coach in her own business.

Kelly uses proven coaching strategies and evidence-based practices, subscribing to the ICF and Fearless Living™ coaching competencies to coach her clients forward to create the life they choose. She is certified to conduct in-person and online workshops and seminars, in addition to providing highly personalized individual, as well as tailored group coaching. Kelly is dedicated to addressing and reducing the impact of intra- and interpersonal stigma. Her coaching focuses on moving her clients toward reaching their desired goals, on creating and sustaining self-compassion practices, and by encouraging faith in body, heart and soul. Kelly's clients range from staff and patients in medical practices, government and service organizations, to highly skilled artists and other professionals. As part of her ongoing work, Kelly provides coaching and leadership training to people in underserved and stigmatized communities to "pay coaching forward".

Be Fearless in Faith in Your Body, Heart and Soul

By Kelly O'Keefe Voorhees

"There is no fear in love, but perfect love drives out fear." 1 John 4:18

I am a Fearless Living Coach. I help people to find the courage to be who they want to be, even if that involves doing what seems impossible!

If I could give anything to the world, it would be faith. Faith can be spiritual. It can also be belief in yourself that you are created whole and can achieve what your heart desires.

I have privilege. It is what most call "white privilege." I was also privileged to be diagnosed with a mood imbalance when I was 16 years old. I didn't think so at the time, I didn't know then that about 5% of me is "over seasoned" or "under seasoned" at times. I live with a mood imbalance that encourages me to strive for balance. Nearly 100% of the time my life is well-seasoned. It's just that 5% of the time when I forget to put the baking soda in the cake, or when I add the extra teaspoon of salt to the soup, and Voila! The end result is not empowering to me or others around me. Yet I carried the severe stigma and shame of being diagnosed with a mood imbalance into my adult years. I continued to hide who I was in body, heart and soul from every person I met. These days I am on a journey to uncover my innocence throughout my life, remembering the hard experiences I have had, and giving myself the privilege to reframe those experiences in love and compassion and gentleness for myself and everyone around me. This is hard and rewarding work! I invite you to come on a Pathstone Meditation Journey of change with me to be more fearless in faith in your body, heart and soul. I am going on this journey to change how I relate to "privilege" in my life. What do you want to change?

Innocence and Forgiveness

When I became a Certified Fearless Living Coach, I learned how to recognize innocence and choose forgiveness for myself. I learned that my soul is love. I realized that I had lost my sanity, self-worth and sobriety to fear of other people knowing who I really was all my life. Through the Fearless Living Training Program, I did the work to find more joy, innocence and forgiveness. I let go of being a victim in my life. I became a victor in my life.

We are free to choose to respond to events, people, and patterns in our lives with forgiveness, with innocence, with compassion for self, and a myriad of other ways. What can this mean in a practical sense, when our first response can be to fight, run away or freeze? I'd like to teach you about a pathway of twelve meditation stones I have used to become more fearless in faith in my body, heart and soul. This can show you how you can master change in your life and avoid the very common instinct to fight, flight or freeze when faced with the choice to make a change.

In the Pathstone Meditation Journey, one of the tools I use is Rhonda Britten's 12 Fearless Principles found in her course Pathway of Change™.

While studying to become a Certified Fearless Living Coach, I took the Pathway of Change™ course that shared 12 Fearless Principles. I fell in love with the simplicity and specifically the order in which they deepened my faith, and how they profoundly supported me to change my life. Soon, I began to use the Fearless Principles as my foundation on what I call the Pathstone Meditation Journey. It is powerful.

Let me show you how I like to think of each Fearless Principle as a stone on my path, where I can stop and reflect upon my process and intention for change. For this meditation of change, I have created my own set of twelve stones plus an Intention touchstone that represent the order I have chosen for this particular journey. Each stone has an accompanying meaning that can be used for meditation. I describe meditations based on what I learned as a Fearless Living Trainer in the Pathway of Change™ course. I also provide movements you can use in your meditation to become more aware of your body during this journey. Allow yourself to sense changes within and around you! The following represents an example of a pathway to change. If you find this pathway appealing, I can help coach you through these steps of change.

Pathstone Meditation Journey

Imagine you are setting out on a journey to a completely new destination. You want to make a change in your life. What are you feeling? Excitement? Trepidation? Are you ready to go? Do you really just want to stay where you are? The path ahead is your choice- you might choose to walk, or run, or lie down. You can sit in your chair and move through this journey in your mind, you can write your experience in your journal, or on your computer. You can sit and listen to someone read this meditation to you. Your path is up to you. Always.

Intention

Touchstone Golden Onyx: Inner strength, self-mastery

One hand over abdomen and one hand just below belly button.

Before you begin your meditation journey to change, you must create your starting point. This is your Intention Statement. Your Intention is critical for success, it lays the foundation for change. It alerts your subconscious mind that things are about to change, and when your mind starts to wander, your Intention Statement will keep you grounded. It begins with the stem sentence "I am willing to practice…." To create your Intention Statement, think of what qualities would best support you to make the change you want. Are you willing to practice Courage? Focus? Accountability? Authenticity? Also, who are you willing to be to effect the change you want in your life? Open or closed? Teachable or unteachable? Committed or uncommitted? Vulnerable or guarded? Are you willing to step out of your comfort zone to create change? A Fearless Living Intention is a proactive statement that excites you, empowers you, challenges you, and inspires you to take action. Here's an example: "I am willing to practice having an open heart and open mind over the next twelve pathstones of this meditation." Or "I am willing to practice being accountable to myself and others." My own intention is this: "I am willing to practice justice toward myself and my fellow sisters and brothers." When you have created your Intention, you are ready to step onto the first pathstone of Awareness.

Your Intention: I am willing to practice
_____.

Fearless Principle #1: Awareness: That something needs to change

Pathstone #1 Black Tourmaline: Purification, protection

Connect soles of feet to the ground, hands gently over heart.

The first stone on the path is Awareness. Change can't happen until we become aware that something needs to change. Where are you most aware of your need to change? Do you feel it in your body? In your heart? Your soul? Settle in to your awareness of your desire to change. You can make a list of all the things you want to change right now: anything. Then, choose one thing to focus on during this Pathstone Meditation Journey. Becoming aware of your one thing to change gives you the power to achieve it. The area of my life that I want to change has to do with my personal awareness and actions: I am willing to learn how to use the word "privilege" differently in my life.

Fearless Principle #2: Willingness: To take action

Pathstone #2 Red Poppy Jasper: Vitality, stability

Open hands in front of your heart, or on your lap.

The second stone on the path is Willingness. When we become willing, we let go of "wanting to" or "having to" do something, and life becomes a process. The definition of willingness is the state of being prepared to do something. It means readiness to accept new opportunities and open pathways, just like the one you are on now. Willingness opens doors for us, and creates more possibilities, solutions, and a way forward. When we are willing, we open our eyes and hearts to others and to ourselves. Being willing sets us free from our past and allows us to become more of who we are meant to be.

Fearless Principle #3: Connection: With self and others to give and receive support

Pathstone #3 Yellow Citrine: Personal will, mental clarity

Send and receive blessings to your heart center.

The third stone on the path is Connection. When our needs for survival and safety are met, our first need is Connection. This is where faith in your body, heart and soul becomes really important. Connection to others is sometimes easier to focus on, and we forget to connect to ourselves, to our body, heart and soul. When our thoughts and feelings are disconnected, we cannot be true to ourselves and we might get caught up in regret or even addictive behaviors. Place your hand over your heart right now, breathe in deeply and send your breath and thoughts of the change you wish to make to your heart center. Connect your "body-breath-heart-mind" to the change you are making on this Pathstone Meditation Journey for five breaths, then sit quietly for a minute or two. Notice what happens.

Fearless Principle #4: Compassion: For yourself and others

Pathstone #4 Pink Rhodonite: Compassion, altruism

Hand over heart center, feel your heart beat.

The fourth stone on the path is Compassion. It is time to be gentle with yourself and others. Time to let go of self-regret and blame. Time to begin to forgive yourself and others on this pathstone. Think about this, how much compassion do you have for your own imperfections? I lived my life believing that my mood imbalances made me 100% imperfect! I could not love anyone else, or be true to my own soul, because I could not love myself. What could you do to increase compassion towards yourself? What stops you from having compassion for others? How will having compassion for others benefit you? Remember, this work of change is hard AND rewarding!

Fearless Principle #5: Accountable: To self and your healing process

Pathstone #5 Green Fluorite: Healing heart, focus

Open your arms wide and sweep love into your heart.

The fifth stone on the path is Accountable. The change you want to see happen will come when you can say, "That was no longer who I chose to be. This is who I choose to be." Be accountable to yourself and your healing process as your desire to create change brings up secrets you thought had disappeared. Here is where we can be honest with ourselves and tell ourselves the truth. We are on our journey to freedom. On this stone I realize how much my own privilege has destroyed the hopes and dignity of so many people on my life path.

Fearless Principle #6: Present Moment: Remembering this is all we have

Pathstone #6 Orange Carnelian: Courage, confidence, action

Place both hands over your belly button.

The sixth stone on the path is Present Moment. Now it is time to get centered again, to take the effort to focus on the PRESENT MOMENT RIGHT NOW. The past is in our mind and the future is not here yet. To realize the change you want to see, staying in the Present Moment makes it easier to let go of what "should be" and embrace "what is". You are creating your future right now, by how you live in this exact moment. Focus on the warmth of your hands over your abdomen and be in the Present Moment. With purpose ground yourself into "What is, right now." What is my own privilege at this very moment in time? I have become more aware of where I am standing!

Fearless Principle #7: Surrender: Who you are and currently what is

Pathstone #7 Blue-gold Labradorite: Change, protection

Instead of "taking a breath"-- feel yourself breathing your body.

The seventh stone on the path is Surrender. Surrender, acceptance and forgiveness go together. When we let go of judging ourselves, we can be and do what was impossible before. Surrendering is about letting go of what you think "should change" for "what is possible". When you surrender, you give up control and yield to something greater and allow your change to happen. You practice complete acceptance of "what is"; and you practice living in faith that "all is well". Here is a Fearless Living Fearbuster Exercise™: Take two 3x5 cards. At the top of one write "I am willing to forgive." At the top of the other one write "I am willing to surrender." Think about what you are willing to do, let go of, think, say or anything else, to achieve the change you wish to see in your world. Fill up both cards. Allow yourself to feel what you have written in whatever way works for you. Then let go of what you have written on the cards: tear them up, burn them, destroy them. Surrender who you think you are in order to embrace who you can become.

REST STOP: What are you beginning to realize about your Pathstone Meditation Journey?

On this Pathstone Meditation Journey, I am beginning to realize that my definition of privilege is changing. I am surrendering to and accepting my own definition of privilege and what I can now do to create blessings for every person I meet.

Fearless Principle #8: Possibilities: Opening up to what can be

Pathstone #8 Rose Quartz: Love, gentleness, emotional healing

Create your rainbow path: sweep blessings side to side above head.

The eighth stone on the path is Possibilities. Congratulations! You have surrendered who you thought you were. You've let go of the old and are open to new Possibilities. Now your change process can become as energized and motivated and inspired as you have become! Any change you wish to see is possible because the word "no" doesn't stop you anymore. This is the time to brainstorm, to write down all the possibilities that you envision, and celebrate your new position of living in Possibilities. Draw a picture for yourself of what is possible now that you have surrendered the old to embrace the new. Place this picture where you can see it every day.

Fearless Principle #9: Intention: Focusing forward

Pathstone #9 Blue Apatite: Access to knowledge

Bring open palms over head, pull all wisdom into your heart center

The ninth stone on the path is Intention. An Intention is a proactive statement, like the one you wrote to focus your journey forward. It is written in the present moment, and it is supported by goals. Intentions help us to focus our possibilities to filter out what may not move us toward the impactful change we are planning to achieve. What are you willing to practice to move you toward the change you are creating, and what goals will support you to get there? An intention is a quality of being, like "I am willing to practice compassion for myself and others." And goals are actions that support your intention, such as, "I will listen to my friend's points of view for 3 minutes before speaking." Or "I will ask ten friends what the word privilege means to them and write their answers down in my journal."

Fearless Principle #10: Trust: Yourself and your decisions

Pathstone #10 Deep Blue Lapis Lazuli: Inner vision, truthful communication

Gently tap the spot between your eyebrows, with eyes focused downward.

The tenth stone on the path is Trust. What does it mean to trust yourself? Is it harder to trust yourself or someone else? Trusting yourself comes naturally when you live by your chosen Intention. Some of the benefits of trust are that it expands your world and opens your heart to change. Place your hand over your heart- where can you feel trust in yourself? Does this feel the same, different or something else when compared to Pathstone #3 of Connection when you placed your hand over your heart to connect to yourself and others? Consistent words and deeds are the key to creating trust in others, and in yourself. How can trusting yourself open your heart to change? The answers to trusting change are within yourself. I am beginning to trust how awareness of my own privilege is connected to every person I meet.

Fearless Principle #11: Passion: Fuels your journey

Pathstone #11 Purple Amethyst: Purification, divine connection

Send your blessings out to all corners of the world.

The eleventh stone on the path is Passion. Passion can save or destroy the world, and maybe it does both. True passion is about being the real you, cracks and all, and shining your brightest self for everyone to see. Most of us are scared of passion- we are afraid it will come out too strong or too weird or not be politically correct. People who look for the good in every situation and are grateful for the everyday gifts live in passion. Living in passion also means living in the present moment, open to all possibilities, focused on your intention, and practicing absolute trust in yourself. Passionate people take risks, they take action, they make change happen. I send my blessings out to the world, asking others what their privilege is in this moment.

Fearless Principle #12: Love: Yourself

Pathstone #12 Clear Quartz: Amplification of one's intention, healing

Send your blessings out to all corners of the universe.

The twelfth stone on the path is Love. Love is the last pathstone on this meditation journey. Love contains vulnerability, strength, courage and compassion. Love helps us experience connection with ourselves and others. We are able to know our boundaries. Love is everything. How do you know you love yourself and you are walking in love? You are gentle with yourself. You consider others' thoughts and feelings. You let others into your world without fear of reprimand, for you trust yourself. You love passionately without thought or need for return. Loving yourself through change begins when you begin to be fearless in faith in your body, heart and soul. At the end of this Pathstone Meditation Journey, I now ask, "What steps do I now take to begin to create more privilege for my sisters and brothers?"

All these stones are tied together on one path, from your awareness of your desire to change, to loving yourself in the change you have made. As one meditation stone follows the other, allow your faith to take you through these steps one by one when you want to make a change in your life. Feel free to change the order and type of stones on your own meditation journey to suit your chosen path and desire for change.

Be Fearless in Faith in Your Body, Heart and Soul

My vision is a world where you are able to practice your faith as you choose. My mission is to support you to be fearless in faith in your body, heart and soul. Through coaching, I can support you to create the change you want in your life. Be willing to learn that your body, heart and soul are completely connected to who you are, just like the pathstones on this meditation journey.

You can change our world.

References

NIV Faithlife Study Bible, (Lexham Press, 2017; NIV: Zondervan, Grand Rapids, MI. 2011).

Fearless Living, Rhonda Britten, (Perigee Books, 2011).

Self-Compassion, Kristin Neff, (Harper-Collins, 2011).

Pathway of Change™: *Pathway of Change is a trademark of Rhonda Britten and the Fearless Living Institute, Inc. Fearless Living is a trademark registered in the US Patent and Trademark Office.*

***

To contact Kelly:

Email: Kelly@coachforward.com

Website: www.coachforward.com

LinkedIn: www.linkedin.com/in/kellyvoorheescoach/

Jim Cocks

After what Jim likes to call his "quarter life crisis", he began his journey as a coach, his mission, to impact as many lives as possible. Recently featured in Australia's Best Business Coaches, with over 15 years of experience in Sales, Marketing and Leadership across multiple industries, Jim found his calling coaching fellow coaches and experts to grow and scale their businesses to create massive success. "I want to impact as many lives as I can through the power of coaching. By coaching other entrepreneurs, I have the opportunity to impact so many more lives than I ever could on my own."

An Entrepreneur's Biggest Challenge – Get Out of Your Own Way

By Jim Cocks

Self-defeating behaviour is one of the biggest things holding you back in life. Whether from childhood or passed down from our prehistoric ancestors, we are wired to protect and preserve. The problem with this is we resist change, fear failure and need to push past our pre-programmed patterns to evolve and grow.

I believe entrepreneurs have one of the toughest challenges in life – going against the norm, resisting the easier path of working for someone else, just so you can struggle, fail, cry, start up again, get overwhelmed and break a few things. But then, for those with the courage to never give up, you will find massive success. Success that those too fearful to stray from the path of regular society will never experience themselves.

Before becoming a Business Coach, I failed – A LOT – and if I knew then what I do now, my success would have come so much faster. You can get on the fast-track, eliminate fear, doubt, overwhelm, exhaustion, whatever is holding you back right now, whether you are just starting out or ready to level-up your business. I will reveal how shortly. But first let me tell you a story…

Three years ago, I landed my dream job; a regional role, 6 figure income, the opportunity to reshape the culture of a massive business with an ancient culture that didn't in any way, value its people. I felt like I was going to change the world. I'd made it. I was wrong.

I worked long hours for little result. The business moved slowly and was stuck in a tiresome process, keeping its partners happy, while all I wanted to do was innovate and help people grow. My boss was labelling my work as hers because she was too fearful of who we worked for. That led to attempts to damage my relationship with my team. If you believe you need to stand on someone to look better, you should not be a leader. Mornings came where I struggled to get out of bed. After hitting snooze six times I'd finally shower, get in the car and pull up in the underground, cold, concrete car park next to my office. For me to get the courage to open the door and take on another day, I'd scream at the top of my lungs, already waiting for 5pm to arrive.

Without the mindset, coaching tools or friends I have now and with my family so far away, I fell into heavy drinking, drugs and excessive partying to escape reality. Looking back, I was a zombie, barely treading water, waiting for something to swallow me up. It finally came to a breaking point. I called my parents, quit my job and moved back to my hometown. To this day I don't think I would still be on this planet if I didn't have my amazing family swoop in and rescue me – driving 11 hours in a red mini-van to pack up my belongings and get me home.

For the next 6 months, I'd sit on the couch (if I even got out of bed), watching tv series after tv series. "I could be doing something so much more productive right now". My mind would wander to all the awesome ideas and things I wanted to achieve and then, satisfied that I'd completed some "prep work", I'd go back to what I was watching. "I'll start it tomorrow".

Sound familiar? You know your next big thing is coming, it just hasn't appeared yet. Then the realisation comes. Life won't give you what you deserve, it gives you what you are dedicated to. You have to take action and go out and get it.

Then change came. I found a coach and it was thanks to his guidance that I found my calling. *"I can help people achieve success, create more freedom for myself and earn more in an hour than I did in a day?!"*

I kept the momentum going, enrolled in a Masters program to become a certified coach and started coaching and consulting as soon as I had the tools to help people create positive change.

Soon I discovered that as a Coach there were only so many people I could work with. Group coaching definitely helped increase my reach, but I can't serve everyone because I can't solve everyone's problems. I wanted to share what coaching could do with the world – I just need to figure out how. It was around this time I began to see talented, inspiring Coaches, not achieve the success we had all spoken of when studying together because they simply didn't have the entrepreneurial mindset and clarity in their business strategy to keep going once the study had finished. This is what made me decide to become a Business Coach. Helping others grow their business so that their future clients can find them and impacting more people through coaching than I ever could on my own.

The challenge is uncertainty, doubt, lack of clarity and confidence in taking the next step, whatever level you are at. Creating a change within ourselves to evolve. We are after all creatures of habit and we live by our patterns, whether they serve us or destroy us.

The caveman still lives within us. Our automated protection system also known as the Reticular Activating System is the part of the brain that mediates our behaviour. Helping us feel safe and secure. It definitely has a purpose, otherwise we would probably have a much shorter lifespan. We learn the bulk of our behaviour through our genetics and imitating that of those around us as we grow up. However, the routines we create as adults, continue to shape our journey. Whether good or bad for us, our habits set off a chemical reaction in our bodies – almost like a mini "Whoo-hoo we did it again!"

Where this pattern matching gets detrimental to success, is when our brains begin to reward our self-sabotaging behaviour and limiting beliefs. The first step to changing anything is admitting that change is needed. This doesn't mean altering your identity. However, you do need to alter your actions. Don't be so hard on yourself. That just makes it… well… harder.

For my clients, fellow coaches and business owners, the biggest bad habit I see is procrastination which is caused by fear. This is because this little devil is so good at disguising itself in so many different ways. So now I'm going to reveal to you some of the ways this can show up and, more importantly, how you can overcome it.

Waiting for Perfection

When you run your own business, you must let go of perfection. Whether working alone or in a team, it is always going to be difficult and time consuming to get everything exactly the way you want it to be. On top of this, you are limiting the amount of growth you can obtain from new concepts and ideas. Think of the last time you had a meeting with a client or decided to introduce a new product or service. You had refreshed motivation and felt energised by all the possibilities ahead, then something didn't go the way you'd planned, or you needed to take a new path. The plan you had at the beginning needed to change. Your to do list got longer, then came the overwhelm and soon you wondered if you were ever going to get everything done.

It's important to note that procrastination can be secretly disguised as perfectionism as well. Working a lot with Coaches and Consultants, the biggest example of this I usually see is when it comes to starting something new, "I can't work with that client because I don't have the tools or experience yet" or "No point in marketing my new program until I've created all the content".

The next thing I'm going to say might shock some of you or maybe even scare you, as this seems all wrong! My motto is, "always say yes and work it out later."

There is no point investing your precious time and money in something new if nobody out there is going to pay for it. Further to this, you might discover a new challenge or direction for your business to go in. So, if someone believes you have the skill set to do it and it's something that you would like to pursue, take the opportunity by the horns and figure out how to navigate it! How much money are you leaving on the table because you don't feel you're ready?

Now, I'm not saying go in completely blind. It's important to have a plan or overview when developing a new product or service but first and foremost for any business is: marketing. Marketing brings the customers and you need to ensure you are going to find the right audience that will absolutely love what you do.

If, for example, you are a coach and you spend months developing content for a new workshop or 3 month program, to then discover that nobody wants to purchase it or there's a bigger challenge you can help your target audience with, how much time have you wasted in the process? My recommendation: clearly define your customers' challenge, outline how you are going to overcome it, map out the steps that you are going to take them through, then test and market it with your audience. After all, if you're building a course, you really only need to stay one week ahead of your first client, right? Having someone paying you to deliver, definitely lights a fire up your backside to get it done.

The Information Junkie

I like to call this "Shiny New Thing" Syndrome. There is so much information out there and being a minimalist, I like to have clear focus. However, I love learning about the latest thing or new ways I can help my clients. As such and while I always seek clarity, I get bombarded with new and exciting ideas on an almost daily basis. How many unread messages are in your inbox right now? Ideas, concepts, tools from other coaches, trainers and experts? Maybe you've favourited some because the tag line has appealed to you or you've had a scroll through and think they have something fairly decent to offer. Ask yourself: How often do you actually go back and action them all?

The truth is, information is everywhere. I'm sure you could find articles, interviews, YouTube videos on similar topics to exactly what you are reading now. Despite the fact this is all pouring out of my head does not necessarily mean that no one else has the same idea or opinion. What creates a successful entrepreneur? It's simple really. Action.

You might have collected, collated and categorised all the tools, scripts, templates and ideas in the world to drive your sales and marketing but if you never make an offer to someone, how are you ever going to make a sale? Do yourself a favour and go on an information diet. Hit the unsubscribe button on all those emails that you never really read. Archive all those lists, tools, webinars, ebooks to revisit when they are needed (if they are ever needed again). Commit to one thing, one process, implement it and then move onto the next.

Results do not come when you have all the answers. They come when you are ready to face the tough questions and create action.

What are you scared of? What's holding you back? What will happen if you do make an offer? What will happen if you don't?

Fear of Failure

What belief do you have around the word "failure"? I could throw an inspirational quote out here right now like: "Failures are simply learnings to get you closer to your goals" but we see those plastered everywhere! Dig deeper than you do normally. What are you afraid of right now? Is this fear protecting you from harm or is it protecting you from achieving success? Because that little, grey, almond shaped prehistoric part of our brain called the amygdala, which is responsible for our behaviour and ultimately our safety, can also be responsible for our demise.

We are ever growing and expanding through change, yet so many people out there make a massive amount of income from helping businesses navigate exactly this. Why are people so averse to change if we are doing it constantly?

The truth is, we love routine, we love patterns – so much so, that our brains actually reward us with a little dose of happiness every time we finish a pattern. Just like that bad habit you want to get rid of but haven't yet. Because it's safe right? You've done it before, it made you feel good, let's do it again! On the opposite spectrum there are definitely things you know are good for you, but you simply can't find the motivation to do them.

Our subconscious hates the unknown. We are automated to look for the negative in everything, to keep us safe. Yet when we are growing a business, we need to push through those uncomfortable moments to test new ways of doing things for our businesses to grow and scale.

I hear you saying: "Jim! I get it! But how the hell do I overcome it?" Well that's something you need to ask yourself! I apologise for having a moment of getting coachy with you, but I've already started so I'm going to do it anyway: after all it's what I'm good at. I want you to think of a time that you felt stuck, trapped, overwhelmed and overcame those feelings to achieve success. Take a deep breath and think of a time, a specific time, that you were resisting change and overcame it. What was going on at that time? Were you with anyone when you discovered how to overcome that hurdle? What were you feeling and telling yourself as a result?

See! The truth is you've done it before, and you can do it again. All you need to do is find the right way to go about it, the right mindset, the right support, the right belief that aligns with your values. If you don't know your values, then you definitely need to figure out what they are because they will help you create so much more happiness and success in your life. Think of them as your personal GPS. How annoying is it when you are trying to find an address, you have the map, but you don't have a GPS signal!

So, these are the three key areas I find myself coaching entrepreneurs on the majority of the time. Wherever their business needs work, they are usually in a stuck state and need guidance to ensure they can fast track back to success. This is why I believe coaching is so integral to any entrepreneur, yes, even fellow coaches! While we are great at helping others, it makes it really easy to avoid helping ourselves. I always ensure I'm working with a coach. I definitely factor my own success to having one at hand to slap me out of unwanted states and to be my sidekick to achieving massive results in all areas of my business and my life.

Sometimes, as entrepreneurs, we need to take a step back and ask, "Would I fire me?" I know it sounds harsh but when you take the leap to go out on your own and rock your own business world, who's there to performance manage you? Your clients might know you through a product or service you are providing but they don't see the whole picture. Frequently take stock and assess where you are at in each segment of your business.

One way I do this with clients is through what I call "The Unstoppable Wheel". Draw a circle on a page and split it into eight sections. What I want you to do is label each section as a component of your business: Sales, Marketing, Service, Technology and Systems, People and Culture, Legal, Operation, Finance.

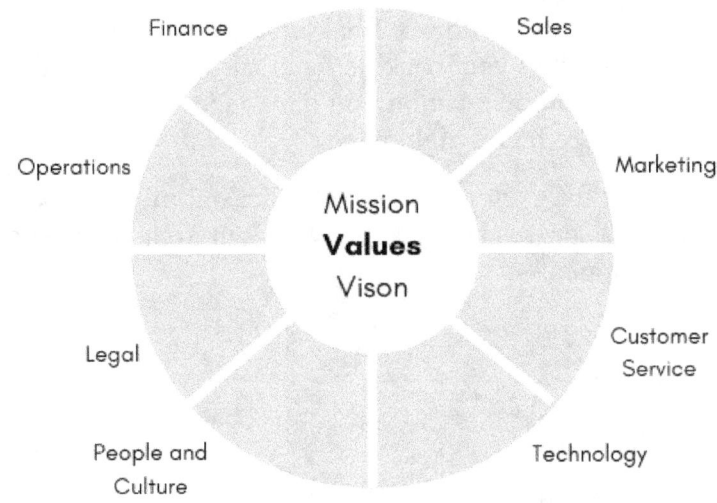

The Unstoppable Wheel™
Clear Edge Coaching

From here you then look at each segment and rate yourself between 0-10 on how satisfied you are with that component of your business. Once you have that number, draw a line through that section of the wheel. You'll find by the time you work your way around the entire wheel you will have a clear visual on how you are tracking and where you need to focus your attention next.

I want to leave you with a little secret weapon that I use constantly to shake my own unwanted habits. Stop saying "I am" and start saying, "I'm doing". As an example, stop saying, "I'm a perfectionist" and start saying, "I'm doing perfection right now." Labelling yourself subconsciously makes the state a part of your identity and this is much harder to change. From here, identify your triggers and you will find it easier to break the pattern with a little bit of willpower. Remember your subconscious really, REALLY wants to complete this pattern the way it always has. It knows that doing so will give you that hit of endorphins.

There is so much more I'd love to share with you, I truly believe success comes so much easier when you don't do it alone and if anyone can learn from my own failures I want to bare it all! Without any embellishments and nothing hidden behind the curtain. For now though, I hope you have taken something away from this chapter and I want to leave you with one final remark. The only person that is ultimately holding you back is yourself, take responsibility, whatever the situation, an action you have taken has gotten you to the challenge you're facing right now.

My mantra: Get the f*ck over yourself. Get out of your own way. Take action and be ready, because you will find more success, freedom and happiness.

***

To contact Jim:

info@clearedgecoaching.com

www.clearedgecoaching.com

www.leveluptribe.com

https://www.linkedin.com/in/jim-cocks-clearedgecoaching/

Kim Levings

Kim Levings is an immigrant from South Africa, arrived in the USA in 1993. After more than fifteen years' experience in Human Resources and Manpower Development in South Africa with some of the country's largest retail and manufacturing organizations, Kim founded her own consulting firm in west Los Angeles and provided training product development, facilitation, organizational design, and coaching for businesses and churches/ministries. Kim was instrumental in the development of the training and coaching materials for the original founder of the technology now used by ThinkX and has been an advocate and provider of the solutions for more than 25 years.

Kim is a master trainer and coach with expertise in strategic human capital development, performance systems, performance coaching, behavioral skills training, and career/life skills coaching. Her personal mission is to help people excel at their desired goals and careers. Kim assumed several key executive roles with privately owned companies (clients), alongside her own consulting and coaching business in California and Colorado. Kim is passionate about helping leaders build high performing companies that results in healthy employees and work culture.

Kim has studied in the fields of psychology and organizational development, and pursued a Bachelor of Commerce degree, part time, majoring in industrial psychology. She currently resides in Colorado Springs and when not traveling to beautiful places around the world, she enjoys having time with her family and wonderful network of friends.

Ted Malley

Ted Malley is the Chairman of the Board at ThinkX with over 25 years of experience as a senior executive in the technology industry and over 20 of those years in the Human Capital Management software business. As the former Chief Customer Officer at Ceridian, Ted combined his personal passion for helping people and love for new technology to change the way Ceridian engages its customers using *RelateAbility* principles to build trusting relationships.

Before joining Ceridian, Ted co-founded *RelatedMatters, Inc.* and developed the mobile app *TeamRelate*, which was acquired by Ceridian in March 2015. *TeamRelate* combines mobile technology, social networking, and behavioral science into a powerful communication team engagement tool for today's workforce.

His personal mission is to work with great teams of people who are driven by achievement, not money, and excellence over status and title. His desire is to change the world for the better, one relationship at a time.

Ted holds a degree in Computer Science from Cal Poly, San Luis Obispo, CA and loves spending time with his wife and 4 children in Arroyo Grande, CA.

If you could think your way to success, why isn't everyone a success?

By Ted Malley and Kim Levings

Being successful often does equate to being rich, granted, but as Zig Ziglar said, "Money isn't everything, but it ranks up there with oxygen." Most times the amount of wealth is correlated with the level of success. Reading this book indicates that you are likely in pursuit of that wealth and want to research every possible method of creating success in pursuit of you dream.

Self-starters, like you, prioritize personal development through absorbing information and learning from multiple sources and mediums. They are the people who know they own their results and are responsible for their own success. You have "ownership" of your life and your outcomes. These are all great starting points. Therein lies the question, though. As Mockridge said to Nygama, "If you're so smart, why aren't you rich?" in the 40th episode of Batman and Robin, in 1992.

If success, ownership, wealth, results, were all direct output of your inputs, then we would all have cracked the Rich Code. We would all know exactly what to do to get what we want. The reality is that we also have barriers to overcome and breakthrough. Our ability to breakthrough barriers is so important. Barriers can exist in various shapes and forms, and the strategy to break through them differs. What works in one area may not work in another. In this chapter we will explain the barriers of the mind, and how to re-frame them, to develop higher level performance thinking.

Understanding the power of thinking

According to the National Science Foundation, an average person has about 12,000 to 60,000 thoughts per day. Of those, approximately 80% of those thoughts are negative and 95% are repetitive thoughts we had the day before. How we think, positively or negatively, has a direct correlation to our attitudes, emotions, and behaviors. Conscious level thought (or "higher level reasoning") is that part of your intellectual self which is responsible for encouraging good behavior that comes from good decisions and choices. This is where information and input of self-development is stored and processed. The next layer down is the sub-conscious layer where memory and emotions are stored and recalled. When you have good feedback and good results from various behaviors and choices, that memory is stored. It is a reward of sort – reinforcing "good" behavior and avoiding "bad" behavior.

Pause for a moment and think about that paragraph. Your brain has just assimilated the information you read and you either agree or disagree with the statements made. As you go through life, wouldn't it be just fabulous if you operated in the higher-level reasoning and memory zones? Absolutely. That would make thinking simple! Unfortunately, you've just examined about 20% of your brain's way of processing. The "tip of the iceberg."

You have an entire lifetime of thinking stored in the sub-conscious brain – the deep, root source algorithms that actually "steer the ship." Alyssa Dver in her powerful book, *Confidence is a Choice, published in 2020,* refers to the sub-conscious brain as the Chief of Staff, and the cortex, conscious brain, as the CEO. The Chief of Staff always knows what's going on – it reads the emotional response to a situation. So, while the CEO may make a good decision and drive a response, the Chief of Staff will often resist, resent, reverse those decisions. The sub-conscious root source thinking is the operating code. It is where your reactivity is sourced, and it comes from previous memory.

Let's look at an illustration of how this may show up:

You have had a good, productive morning of work. You are feeling positive and energetic. You're your body reminds you that it needs some food, and realize its lunch time, so you decide to take a break. As you're to make the salad you had planned, a friend calls you. He is having a lousy day and wants to meet you at the local burger place. You hesitate. The CEO is saying, "No – you don't want to lose your focus, and besides, you don't even like burgers anymore." The Chief of Staff says, "Hey, he's a buddy and I always make people my priority – taking care of others makes me feel good, and I like being needed.* It's just a burger…" This internal conversation happens in milli-seconds. Which brain wins? Well, that would depend on the depth of the "ruts" (establishing patterns) in the root source.

How deep thinking is formed

The sub-conscious brain is not your enemy. It is there to protect you. It does this by forming responses to events as they occur. If the brain feels threatened, it triggers a fear response of fight, flight, or freeze, a concept with which you are probably familiar. Once it has processed whatever that threat was, a "code" (memory of response) gets stored. So, when the same, or similar event happens, the brain pulls out that code and sends it to the conscious brain for a behavioral response or reaction.

In the salad vs. burger example – the behavioral response had nothing to do with the food choice. It had everything to do with the deeply established "rut" (code) in the brain. In this example, that code is – *"I give priority to others because I need to be needed."* While knowing how that code was stored is not always possible, the fact that you can see it, recognize it, and divert it into a new code, in the moment, is the critical forward path to effective thinking.

Breaking through barriers

We have all had a myriad life experiences that form code and responses in our brains. You may even be aware of some of your behavioral "short comings" and when challenged, perhaps have even said, "I've always been like that." Or "We're Italian, we all talk a lot!" Or "That's just who I am, take it or leave it." The longevity, cultural, or habitual defense doesn't always appease others, though. It is a natural response to challenge because we simply don't know any better.

Knowing just how your own brain "code" is working and which of those established, but incorrect, responses are barriers to your success is an important contributor to your success. If you are fortunate enough to have surfaced a barrier thought – *"I give priority to others because I need to be needed,"* you have an opportunity to examine, evaluate, and then re-frame that root source code.

Examine: I have a need to be needed – so I let others take precedent. *(If you can identify where this pattern started, great. If not, don't stress about it.)*

Evaluate:	Is that thought true and does it serve me well? → No – it causes frustration and resentment eventually. Others sometimes take advantage of me as a result.
Re-frame:	Others are important, and my needs are, too.
	It's not selfish to get my own needs met, as long as I'm still caring for others.

If that re-framed thought is repeated out loud several times a day for several weeks, the new "code" is stored in the brain. In effect, you have created a new neural pathway. In the words of Daniel Dennet:

"...consciousness developed as a way to internalize talking to oneself. Speaking words triggers parts of the brain involved in moving the diaphragm, tongue, lips, vocal chords, etc. Hearing words triggers parts of the brain connected to the ears. Speaking aloud can be a bad survival strategy, especially when you are thinking about the chief's wife, so we developed consciousness as an internal monologue. It works, but it doesn't exercise as many areas of the brain as speaking and hearing your own words." (Consciousness Explained, 1991)

Now, apply that new code into the same situation…your response might be:

"So sorry to hear that you're in a bad place, and I absolutely want to help you through that. I am focused on a project for the next few hours. Can we maybe connect over coffee later, instead?"

Then, eat the salad that serves the body and mind well – get your focus back, while still caring for your friend.

This example is focused on only one barrier, and one thought. There are multiple accelerators and brakes in the way we think. Knowing how to leverage the accelerators and re-frame the thoughts that form brakes is a foundational element of personal growth so essential to be successful.

What thinking supports success?

The ability to understand and access root source thinking is an important breakthrough in establishing and improving the foundations of healthy thinking. Examining and evaluating a set of behaviors, choices, or mindsets that give the possibility of success, will not necessarily deliver the ingrained thought processes that will indeed drive successful outcomes. Simply giving individuals a set of tools, or even encouraging them to change mindset, will not necessarily drive changed behavior either.

When you spend the time[1] to develop new thinking and establish the neural pathways that support the desired behavior, long term adoption of new skills and behavior becomes established and sustained over time. This is especially true when the incorrect thinking has been accurately diagnosed, and interventions are laser-focused on those patterns causing barriers to desired, preferred behavior.

After years of applying accurate root source thinking measurement and targeted performance coaching, the ThinkX team have established some common themes around what drives success and what hinders it. We coin the term "ThinkX Behavior" to quantify a collective list of behavioral outcomes that are sourced in a specific thinking pattern. ThinkX behavior is rooted in reality, it results in a healthy sense of self, and creates a pattern of independent motivation and confidence. Think(y) behavior is the opposite. Think(y) behavior is rooted in fear, creates insecurity, and is manifested in prideful, demanding attitudes that arise from having unrealistic expectations. No matter where you might currently place yourself on these scales, identifying the actual root source thinking that is accelerating or hindering your performance is a critical starting point toward sustainable development of successful entrepreneurialism.

---

[1] ThinkX Targeted Coaching delivers thinking shifts in 4-6 weeks on average.

How Root Source Thinking Impacts Behavior

Below is list of various activities. For each, we have described a small list of possible behaviors, which is different, as determined by root source thinking.

Communication

ThinkX Behavior
- Thinks before they speak. Listens carefully.
- Open to others input, and don't feel the need to dominate conversations.
- Learns from others by asking questions.
- Open-minded and curious.
- Enjoys communicating with others.

Think(y) Behavior
- Feels the need to position themselves as more important, and right, about most things.
- Dominates conversations and often speaks over other people.
- Assumes people understand them – so they don't close communication loops.
- Closed-minded and self-righteous.

Managing Expectations

ThinkX Behavior
- Have realistic expectations of what can really be achieved in the moment.
- Balanced approach between pushing for results and slowing down to empower those around them.
- Knows when to slow down, and when to speed up. (High self-awareness)
- Mindful of strengths and their limitations, and those of their teams.

Think(y) Behavior
- Have unrealistic or overly demanding expectations of themselves and others.
- Creates stress and pressure within and with those around them.

- Judgmental and critical when things don't go their way. Reactive and get angry and/or frustrated easily.

Handling Problems

ThinkX Behavior
- Acknowledges challenges and thinks through solutions.
- Finds it easy to navigate through a problem by creative thinking and realistic assessment of solutions.
- Commits to solving problems as they arise.

Think(y) Behavior
- Reactivity can create anger toward a problem, which may block creative solution seeking.
- Blames others and/or circumstances – gets stuck in the loop of complaining.
- Takes longer to solve problems and may even avoid them.

Building & Nurturing Relationships

ThinkX Behavior
- Sees, understands, and accepts the diversity of people around them.
- Open to others' ideas and suggestions.
- Empathic and a good listener – engages with others in humility.
- Closes communication loops and checks for understanding.
- Trusted and liked by others.

Think(y) Behavior
- Can be judgmental and critical of others.
- Prideful and stubborn – will not own their mistakes.
- Find it difficult to build lasting relationships.
- Often upsets others without realizing it.
- Doubting of self, which can manifest as pride and self-centeredness.
- More concerned with self than others – so not trusted or accepted easily.

Ownership

ThinkX Behavior

- Accepts that they own their lives, their thinking, and their results.
- Independent, take charge individuals who make decisions and pursue goals.
- Owns up to mistakes or errors – apologizes and learns from them.

Think(y) Behavior
- Blames others and external circumstances for things that don't go well.
- Can sometimes adopt a learned helplessness -making excuses for lack of results.
- Expects others to support them but offer nothing in return.

Risk & Failure

ThinkX Behavior
- Willing to take calculated risks in pursuit of personal goals.
- Learns from failure and moves on.
- Separate who they are from what they do, so mistakes and failures don't impact their self-esteem.

Think(y) Behavior
- Avoids risk, as they don't want to fail.
- Become challenge-avoidant, to maintain "safe" status quo.
- Blames others for mistakes.
- Labels themselves negatively. Attaches personal identity to their contributions.

Emotional Intelligence

ThinkX Behavior
- Engaging communicator who is highly expressive.
- Caring and compassionate – displays natural empathy toward others.
- Highly aware – High EQ

Think(y) Behavior
- Communicate to "sell" their ideas and their personal sense of identity.
- Self-centered, unaware of the needs or feelings of others.
- Fearful of engagement – Low EQ

Work Approach

ThinkX Behavior
- Takes charge, sets goals, "gets on with it" with minimal supervision.
- Knows and owns their sense of contribution to the larger goals and success of their company/employer.
- High ownership in results – naturally motivated and committed.

Think(y) Behavior
- Tends to be a follower and will wait for direction or instruction.
- Does enough to avoid conflict but shows no ownership for long term results.
- Blames and criticizes, complains, and resists.
- Sees reasons for avoidance, rather than commitment.

Ideation & Creativity

ThinkX Behavior
- Holds loosely onto ideas – doesn't attached identity or esteem.
- Listens to and encourages ideas form others.
- Willing to pivot and re-think when circumstances require it.

Think(y) Behavior
- Attaches identity to their ideas which makes them resistant to input from others.
- May get "stuck" in a rut due to resistance to change or accept new ideas.
- Resists the need to change when circumstances require it.

You may have already put yourself into one or the other category as you read this list. Perhaps even with a higher than normal level of self-awareness and honesty, you identify with some of the Think(y) behavior, too. In our experience, most people are already aware of their less than favorable behavior patterns. Where you currently live in this spectrum is not the issue. It is merely a starting point.

Consider doing the development work and progressing in your thinking.[2]

---

[2] ThinkX Inc. has resolved this dilemma, with the *Px-12 Performance Profile* – which measures the root-source "code" behind thinking, and Targeted Coaching – which specifically, and accurately, empowers you to develop new neural pathways in specifically identified areas of performance barriers. The profile gives the individual an accurate "picture" of the "accelerators" and "brakes" directly impacting how they think. Go to **ThinkXGo.com** for more information.

A Glimpse into the life of a Think(y) Leader

Marcy is a smart engineer who runs a business designed to provide virtual building design systems to architects and industrial engineers. She has a team of 25 and the company, after two successful years of growth and success, has hit a plateau and Marcy is starting to experience turnover. Her people are burned out and tired, and no longer interested in going the extra mile. In exploring this, Marcy is told that she is demanding and often critical of their ideas. They are also tired of her taking the credit for all the success but blaming everyone else when things go wrong. Marcy's head of Sales, Jim, even told her about times when she overlooked people who desperately needed some caring and helpful feedback. Marcy got angry and resistant to this feedback – immediately regretting the fact that she went asking for it. After several days of complaining and internalizing all this stress, she decides to layoff all those who were not doing things the way she wanted them done. "I'm making clean start and will find people who can get the job done!" (Not sure how this story ends – or can you guess?)

A Glimpse into the life of a ThinkX Leader

Joe is a ThinkX leader. He's the founder of a new supply-chain technology that can revolutionize retail stocking systems. Joe had a team of five people helping him in the startup phase, and now, at year 5, he has nearly 75 employees in various teams. Joe keeps a matrix structure in place and encourages cross-pollination of ideas in regular creating sessions. He is also known for his regular investment of time and energy into the nurture of new trainees. During a new product launch, Joe heard that his head designer, Pete, had taken seriously ill and while the team were covering for him, the project was at risk for missing the deadline. Joe took time to speak to Pete and assure him to take the time to get well. He then spent extra hours on the project himself and called the affected client to explain the necessity of a delay in delivery. Joe owned the project and engaged help from others who were willing to do so. When Pete came back to work – he was astonished to see that the project was completed and delivered.

We are sure you recognized these patterns from others you have come across in your own career.

A bit like a fish trying to describe water (the analogy coined by Edgar Schein to describe culture) how we think requires the same brain doing the thinking. Is that a thing? Yes – it would be called "meta" thinking – thinking about thinking. **One of the most sought-after mind hacks is understanding who you are and why you make the choices you do.**

Dr. Carol Dweck has spent over 30 years in classrooms researching the impact of a growth mindset and the power of our positive thinking. Regardless of the subject matter or life situation, a learner's mindset (growth vs. fixed) is ultimately the greatest determinant of success. If a learner is motivated and believes they *can* learn, then they are more likely *to* learn. If a person who aspires success believes that they can become successful through hard work and learning from failure, they are much more likely to actually succeed than a person who believes that success comes more from a particular set of life circumstances.

This is another illustration of how the power of subconscious thinking impacts your behavior. On a leadership level, if leaders can effectively create the thinking that turns their organizations into hyper-learning machines, then this may yield the most significant impact on overall organizational success.

Bottom line - it is possible to "crack the code" that drives success for some individuals and not others.

To contact Ted and Kim:

https://www.linkedin.com/in/kimlevings/

Kim.Levings@ThinkXGo.com

www.linkedin.com/in/tedmalley

Ted.Malley@ThinkXgo.com

www.ThinkXGo.com

Email: Connect@ThinkXGo.com

Princess Merrilee of Solana

A leader in love. Miss Merrilee is an author, imagineer, intuitive relationship expert, counselor, listener, dreamer, and solutions expert. She's a force of nature, in tune and on a mission to demonstrate and inspire the Power of Love. Her life education is what you always needed but never knew existed. Blessed with an unparalleled understanding of the complexity of life, she is lovingly referred to as the Queen of Hearts. Miss Merrilee is the author and master of "The Game," a manual for personal empowerment and character development where love is always the answer.

Princess Merrilee of Solana is recognized by the state of Grace and holds the appointed 8 Point Star Sheriff's badge crowned with the Republic, 8-point star St. Patricks's Commercial Trading Bank Flag under the Kings Bench Magistrate Court Authority. She is ambassador to all countries and islands appointment. Princess Merrilee of Solana is Queen of Camelot.

Why Love is Always the Answer

By Princess Merrilee of Solana

In book one of <u>Cracking the Rich Code; The Esoteric Entrepreneur</u>, I made a point to illuminate the obvious, however these subtly esoteric personality traits that are often taken for granted. Either you have it or you don't, right? Maybe? When we have the self-awareness to consider and reflect on what we're missing, we can absolutely change the fabric of our personality. We need only make a decision and hold ourselves accountable to our commitment.

The question becomes, do I want to be described as having these types of qualities? What a valuable question. Self-awareness is the key to abundance. The next step in creating your abundance will prove to be magical should you decide to make a commitment to its fulfillment. Unlike working hard for every dime and being exhausted from the struggle that most are trained to follow, you can take a different route that's more user friendly and aligned with universal laws. The following stories depict two very different ways of living. Both are very true. *How you get to the end of your treasure depends on which story resonates with your heart*. Please consider carefully as each day is a gift that requires purposeful contribution.

The story of Robert

Robert is in his last year of grad school, sitting in a chair in the back of the room. It's been a long four years. Now that he's closer, he finds himself daydreaming about all the money he plans to make after he earns his cap and gown. He's been planning this day for as long as he can remember. Robert's dad set the pace by grooming him for the best schools and promising him a job with great pay upon graduation. He's imagining the suit and tie, a home with a picket fence complete with a beautiful wife cooking his dinners. Off to work as every man should, proud of himself for being able to support his family. With excitement and a smile, his heart is filled when he sees that boxer puppy running to the door to greet him. He can't wait for life to begin after the years of study and personal sacrifice to live the life he's been dreaming. Thinking back, he is reminded of Elise. She was his high school sweetheart. The memory puts a smile on his face. She was a girl that was so easy and carefree. She loved him so much and never asked for anything. They spent a couple of years together, but college took a toll as most of his time was spent focusing on his goals. He didn't talk much about a future together with her. Eventually she thought it was best to walk away from their relationship. Robert was ok with her decision, figuring there were more women he had yet to meet that might be more suited for him. He was right, there were many women to choose from, but he couldn't afford to give them too much attention. Each encounter failed to last more than a couple of months. He wasn't worried, he still has plenty of time to meet the right girl. But graduation came and went faster than he thought. It was time to get to work. Robert was introduced to many people through his dad's professional network. It didn't take long for him to get hired because of his diploma and a good word.

It's been four years since he graduated. Now sitting at his desk, he wonders if this is all there is and when will it get better. With money in the bank, a secure job and an apartment of his own, he feels the tug at his heart missing the dream he's not yet realized. He still has plenty of time to achieve what he wants, he thinks, so he puts those feelings aside. Instead he makes a shift in his career. Robert follows the call of an entrepreneur. After six months of investing his time, effort, and resources in pursuing a dream of unlimited income, his commitment is now looking a bit fuzzy. This is not as easy as he thought, even with a degree and the support from his dad if he needed it. How was he to know that all of the components he needed to achieve success, would rely on the integrity of others in order to move him up the ladder to abundance? He wasn't prepared to invest so much time and effort networking with so many people, weeding out those he could trust from those only looking to feed off his success. Robert realized it was difficult to discern who was trustworthy and who wasn't when he saw the enthusiasm his prospects showed as he approached them. Every time he thought he could rely on someone he was disappointed by the promises they failed to deliver. How was he to survive investing his money, time, and energy again and again only to be disappointed in the delivery? Each time it seemed the same as he realized his prospect wasn't truly committed. It took a few years to fasten his grip on his business. It wasn't easy to accept that no one is your friend because everyone is focused on the money.

Twenty years pass, Robert sits in his chair reflecting on his decisions. "What's it all about" he thinks to himself, as he hears a car pulling up in the driveway. It's his ex-wife with the kids. The sound is another reminder of the disappointment he carries. He lost the house with the fence after the divorce. The marriage lasted only eight years, when his wife had enough of his neglect and absence from him in their family life. Didn't she understand he was doing the best he could to provide the house with the fence for all to be happy? Now when the kids come to visit, they just sit and watch TV. while he works from home, still buried in his routine, never knowing exactly how to build a relationship with the people he loves. Many years have passed, but at last he can say that all those years of trial, error and sacrifice, built a business that provided many jobs for others. Yes, he's the head of a major corporation where he is responsible for the wealth of the business. His employees are very grateful for their jobs and Christmas bonuses, but yet at the end of each day he sits alone in his office ruminating about all the relationships he sacrificed. No amount of money can replace the life he didn't live. Where did the time go? Robert didn't realize that each day he chose to focus on the money, was a day lost in building his legacy of love. The mother of his children remarried, his kids grew up and now have a life of their own. His parents are gone, and his siblings don't talk very often. All the people, partners and connections he made over the years are no longer, or if they are, they are now just part of operations. If only he knew then what his life would be like now; that all his struggle and sacrifice would produce no guarantee for personal happiness - when time becomes precious and money becomes automatic. Why... with all his education, experience and success, would he be unfulfilled at the end of his life? Maybe because being rich is not about having money?

The story of Elise

It was a beautiful sunny, late fall day in September. Elise just celebrated her ninth birthday. It was a quiet celebration, just her and her mother. Elise is an only child. She spends much of her time alone entertaining herself with music, sewing, dance, and pondering her dreams with her dog Daisy. She had plenty of time to think and just be, without any pressure from her mother regarding her goals, plans for education, profession or money. She lived a simple and comfortable life, knowing her mom loved her and if she ever had a problem, her mother told her to "let go and let God."

As an only child, Elise was very independent. She had many friends all through school, being popular for her smile and friendly personality yet she never quite fit in to any one particular group of people. Her independence was evident in every part of her life. She graduated both high school and college with the same sunny disposition, independent from following the crowd and the normal celebrations.

When it was time to get a job and earn some money, Elise tried many things that just didn't seem to fit her personality nor desire for self-governance. She was fired many times for insubordination. She really didn't know what path she would take or how she would end up making money, but her mother's words clung to her heart; "let go and let god"… and that's exactly what she did. Without a care in the world, knowing she was loved, Elise continued to explore her interest in getting to know herself better. She found what others had to say about her very interesting. Like the pieces to a puzzle, she kept that which fit like a magical narrative.

Just as angels speak through messengers, Elise heard their voices telling her she was special and special she was! Like a plan interrupted, Elise was gathering the pieces to her life when it took a turn, unexpectedly. He came along and she fell in love. Now her independence was overshadowed by her role as a wife and mother. For the next twenty years she devoted herself to creating the ideal for her husband and children. Life was filled with comfort, security, and love for one another. But the angels started conspiring again. Her family unit was short lived as Elise's heart called for something much bigger. It was time to make a decision. The question became love herself first or negate God's calling to spare the family of the pain destined for her loved ones. Without fear, she chose to follow her mother's words to "let go and let god." So, she did and followed her heart's calling.

Now on her own and free to make every decision independent of anyone's opinion, she continued to be happy and grateful, remembering not to worry when life's challenges got heavy. God is in the details she thought. For today, she had everything she needed.

Elise lived everyday with the same sunny outlook that *everything would be provided*. Every day she was proven to be right. This gave her the comfort and the courage to push her dreams further as she tested God's promise. Would He deliver? She wanted to know the plan He had for her, so she continued to love harder. No matter what the challenge or injustice, Elise would continue to prove herself worthy of the gift He said she could not conceive. *All she needed to do was to keep loving.* That's what she did, and life became much more interesting. She was given many tests to pass to see if her commitment was true. She suffered betrayals and losses of great magnitude but with each test she had found the key that helped her pass with flying colors. The key was love and the lock was people.

Elise knew that no matter how dire the situation, or how ominous the consequences, her way out was to love her way through it. Each day became a magical existence as she learned to play with her virtues and not break any rules. To her amazement like magic, people were brought to her life that provided maps to her desires. Just like scripture said, "ask and you shall receive," "believe and you'll move mountains." With every confirmation, her desires got bigger and bolder. How far could she take her dream, she thought. It didn't take long for her to realize that her only boundary was the limitation of her imagination. That's when her dreams really started to come together.

Looking back on earlier days, she could hear the voices from the angels guiding her direction. She was different from the rest, which explained her independence. People in high positions would tell her "we know you're qualified, but we don't know exactly where you're best suited." She didn't know how to take that remark, but it stuck with her knowing there must be a special role in life meant just for her. It was the same in many situations. With each piece of the puzzle, it became apparent that it was love that shined so bright to others, but she didn't know it. Her discovery put her on a very intentional path. Each day she would find or create opportunities to prove evidence that her storybook life was indeed real. Like magic the universe smiled and played along, giving her clues and confirmations each time she recognized the test. Like a child playing in the garden, her games freed her mind from the fears that most others suffer from without them knowing it. The unknown future was the cause of worry, illness, and misbehavior. Elise knew that love was the answer to all of it. That's when the Heavens opened up and told her the role that was best suited for her. To her amazement and delight, all she had to do was live it. With each day, she purposely made a point to carry out her role and make note of it. She would teach the world of her discovery and the power of love.

What a gift she thought, to be the one responsible to deliver the key to relieve the world's misery. But how would it be done and what would be the instruction? Elise knew the answer would be provided after she unlocked enough gates with the key to love that she was gifted. As she played, her days were spent balancing two different worlds. One would provide the tests, the other would be where she created her life story. To her surprise, the angels would come to visit and show her visions of her life while she lay asleep dreaming. Each dream was depicted from a very high elevation. From high in the tower they told her to dream bigger. Both her days and nights were just as exciting, dreaming by day and dreaming by night. Elise had a playground to play in no matter what state of consciousness she lived in. Elise knew what love was and what she was experiencing was a relationship with the Most High. Her life was a gift and she was grateful for every moment.

Then, one special day while playing with a friend, a castle appeared. She knew in her heart it was made especially for her. The story about the purpose of Solana brought tears to her eyes as the plan for its existence was exactly what she had envisioned. The halls were used for meetings to gather great minds to sit and discuss how to make the world better. She held that castle close to her heart making notes in her head on how to tell the story to those who would be interested to inquire. The years passed and her tests became fewer. Now was the time to teach others whatever the question or dilemma, how love was the answer. To her surprise, Elise's blessings grew bigger and incredibly amazing.

Little did she know, with all her good deeds and loving contributions, that the universe was always watching, making plans for her existence. Mountains were moved and planets aligned to a tune that few could ever dare to imagine. Her angels were there to guide her, and special people came to help her up to the Most High dwelling. Elise's commitment to love made her worthy of delivering a message so divine that it could only be sent from the Highest above. It was of such great importance that the message would change the world with each person she told it. What came next was really quite unexpected. The testamentary executor was sent to tell her the special role that was made especially for her. That's how little Miss Elise became a Princess, and everywhere she went, she was welcomed and loved by all who met her.

The story of Robert and Elise are no different from ours. We all have the same decision to make. How will I choose to live my life; will I honor money, or will I honor love?

"No one can serve two masters. Either you will hate the one and love the other, or you will be devoted to the one and despise the other. *You cannot serve both God and money.*"

Matthew 6:24

The Bible says God is love, and there's my choice; love or money. My free will is one choice with everything I do. I chose to love. I made a commitment to let go of all the negative behaviors that came with honoring money; the competition, fear, worry and control. But what does that mean exactly? It meant I had to make an adjustment to my natural method of operation. I, like everyone else, was raised in a world programmed to honor money. My decision was not an easy commitment to keep. I had to learn how to stop feeding my ego with behaviors contrary to honor and integrity. I had to recalibrate my moral compass and reevaluate my expectations. I had to learn how to express myself without hurting others and I had to detach myself from those who didn't hold the same values. I've never looked back since that first day I made my commitment, regardless of the challenge or injustice committed. Over the last ten years of making the same decision to love every day, I have yet to meet one person with the same faith, tenacity, and understanding to do the same. My story is unprecedented because I believed God would deliver as promised. I asked and received. I believed and moved mountains. I don't believe I could have become who I am by navigating on my own. There's no way my life could be what it is if I had made a five-year plan. No, I chose to "let go and let God" (love) guide my direction.

> *"To him who overcomes and does my will to the end, I will give authority over the nations."*
>
> Revelations 2:26

***

To contact Princess Merrilee of Solana:

MerrileeofSolana.com

Merrilee@merrileeofsolana.com

Nadene Joy

CEO of Nadene Joy Consulting Inc, Global Mindset Strategist, Life/Leadership Consultant, Author, Speaker, Certified Psychological Health and Safety Advisor, NLP Practitioner, and Chair/Founder of the Lead 2 Impact Summit

Strategies to Help Business Professionals That are Stuck

By Nadene Joy

Did you know that most leaders and business professionals have gone through times in their lives where they have felt stuck or hit rock bottom? I'm sure you can relate to a business project that just never took off, or a venture that failed, a partnership or relationship that went south, an investment that did not perform or illness that consumed your life? Or maybe you can relate to a time in your life or childhood where you experienced significant loss, grief, pain, disease, heartache, abuse or trauma that you've held onto unknowingly for your entire life? When we go along in life on autopilot, we may or may not recognize that 99% of our thoughts, words and actions are automatically based on unconscious patterns and habits formed from our near or distant past. Unless we become acutely aware of and begin to heal and reprogram what is operating under the surface (or that which may be holding us back from experiencing more out of life), we will reach a plateau in life, in business and in love based on what we were "programmed" to receive and we believe we are worthy of.

Some of the greatest leaders in history grew up in less than ideal circumstances and chose to make a sometimes rather public choice to no longer be held captive by the limitations and demons from their past. They committed to breaking the chains once and for all and to rising above; leading the way for so many others around the world. Martin Luther King Jr. is a prime example of one of the greatest leaders of our time who exhibited true courage and humble leadership, despite the fact that he went through a significant period of horrific discrimination from the time he was a small child. He lived his life in faith and refused to let the system win. He was arrested over 20 times in his lifetime for taking a stand and speaking up for what he believed in. Shockingly, he even had his home bombed, however, despite what most would perceive as obstacles and setbacks, he never gave up on his dream of freedom and hope for all. He showed us our lives must be lived intentionally and without regret, that words mean something, and we must speak up in the face of injustice. He taught us much including that it is one thing to say you have an idea and quite another to act on it. His courageous actions still inspire millions of people today. One of the greatest qualities he possessed was extreme patience, an invaluable virtue indeed.

Nelson Mandela is another prime example of someone who exhibited humility and strength as he endured hardships including being in prison for 27 years under extremely harsh conditions, going through the dark night of the soul and yet he ended up coming out on the other side and never lost his vision and sense of destiny. Don't waste time in illusions and wishes. Take it on and own both the darkness and the light inside of you. Keep your sense of worth, power and vision intact and hold strong in truth. The world desperately needs you to be yourself and value people. Nelson Mandela was aware of the importance of your attitude and fostering relationships when it came to getting unstuck and transforming lives from the inside out. He observed, "You see, when there is danger, a good leader takes the front line. But when there is celebration, a good leader stays in the back room. If you want the cooperation of human beings around you, make them feel that they are important. And you do that by being humble." It's all about valuing others, being appreciative, listening with undivided attention and connecting from the heart.

Maya Angelou is a powerful role model in history on how acknowledging and honouring the dark night (which most times can feel like you are stuck) can lead to a a rebirth and greater newfound presence in the world. She went from not speaking for five or six years as a young child out of guilt and the wounds of severe repetitive abuse to reciting the inaugural poem for Bill Clinton and inspiring millions of others globally to make something of their own dark nights and use it for the greater collective good. She also gained purpose for her own life and inspiration to model the way for many others who felt stuck and haunted by their pasts. Throughout her life and in all her public appearances, Angelou so beautifully and authentically demonstrated both how the pain (dark) and the joy (light) shaped her and other's missions in life. That alone is priceless and something we all can learn from in our own lives.

Pain from Our Past

Did you know that our body holds the pain of our past including imprints from childhood, all the way up to adulthood and up until this present day? Each of the past experiences we have gone through whether positive or negative have been deeply etched into our body, minds, souls and spirits. Those negative experiences are what Eckhart Tolle says are imprinted into "the pain body" which is where we carry all of our painful memories which may eventually show up as imbalance, disease or as a less than ideal version of ourselves.

Struggles, trials and tribulations oftentimes are unexpectedly revealed to us on purpose all according to God's plan to show and teach us more about ourselves and the world in which we live. It is worth noting at this point that our deepest frustrations lead to a place of great transformation and clarity. This "muddy ground" and time of suffering is God's best working ground as it is where we are molded and shaped from the deepest depths within ourselves – growing us in patience, character, endurance, perseverance, and hope. I can guess that many of you reading this chapter, if not all of you, have gone through trials and challenging moments and varying intensities at one point or another in your life. Whether that was abuse, trauma, loss, pain, grief, abandonment, addictions, depression, physical illness or simply thoughts of not being "good enough." We as human beings can relate to suffering and this muddy place that is easy for us to get pulled back into if we're not careful of our thoughts and what we believe as our own truths vs lies others and society have affirmed over us as our misinformed truths, labels, and beliefs that keeps us stuck in a downward destructive cycle vs in an upward constructive forward moving pattern.

How to Most Effectively Move Forward

"When we focus on the past, we can easily become depressed, when we focus on the unknown future we experience anxiety, however, when we choose to focus on the present moment and "just BE," this is where we experience greater peace in all areas of our lives."

It is through living our lives with greater peace, compassion and love in our hearts that we begin to become aligned with our truth. We've all heard the saying "the truth will set you free." Isn't freedom one of the necessities that we long for in our lives? Freedom to be unapologetically you with no masks or alternative agendas or feeling that you need to keep up your facade and image in society based purely on your ego and on what everyone else expects of you. It is this that divides and separates us as a society instead of uniting us closer together. As we align our head(ego) with our hearts(love), we are able to boldly move into our ideal place where we desire that which honours each of us for who we truly are which leads to greater "freedom" for all. It no longer becomes about escaping what we don't want, but rather where we focus intently on the ability to manifest choosing and creating that which we do. Being real, vulnerable, authentic, true to yourself, belonging to a group of like-minded individuals and speaking from the heart is what we search for so deeply in all areas of our lives, including in our business interactions and partnerships. What matters is that we foster relationships where people feel heard, seen and valued and know their voice and opinions matter. Stop for a moment right now to take a few deep breaths and focus on your heart that has been repressed deep within keeping you stuck for a very long time. Usher in complete forgiveness towards yourself and all others who have hurt or wronged you in the past. It is imperative when you do this exercise to include honouring both the painful and joyful parts to our journey. Many times we over complicate life and need to take a step back from a higher "birds-eye" perspective to see how we can simplify, declutter our physical and mental world and clearly become aware of the repressed pain and struggles that may have been lying dormant from the layers of protection and defense mechanisms that were built up over time to protect you from experiencing further debilitating pain. Our past shapes us into the person we are today. It does not define who we are and we always have the choice to choose which path to take in business. Start each day afresh and new. Did you know that all of your subconscious beliefs you have were formed from your experiences and relationships that you developed as a child in between the ages of zero and eight years old? We function most of our lives out of our unconscious subconscious minds based on default patterns from our past experiences. The first step to change in becoming unstuck is creating greater awareness and recognizing that there might be some experiences or events in your life (particularly from childhood) that you have repressed for many years. It is when we begin to see things with greater clarity through the magnifying lens of non judgement and recognize the real pain associated with the event(s) from the past as a profound opportunity to heal and unpack the negative experiences from your suitcase once and for all. One by one we let them go with acknowledgement, grace, compassion and love for ourselves and begin to see the many lessons and blessings that are revealed through this process of unravelling it all bit by bit, layer by layer. It is at this point I promise you will become lighter with every passing day and move closer towards experiencing greater miracles and appreciating the small simple pleasures life has to offer. It is when we open up and share our experiences, trials, tribulations and lessons with others that we begin to inspire many and honour ourselves like never before as we now know and recognize our self-worth and unique place in the world as we have come to learn how to more effectively turn our "mess into our message."

What is one thing you can do right now to get "unstuck"?

It's time to just open up and be real and tell your story without guilt or shame. Look at "accountability" of what you think your life should be and look at and take notice of all the places you are afraid to look at. Acknowledge and accept yourself where you are and choose to no longer be a victim and focus on connection to all through love. As you do this, you develop discernment of where you're at in your relationships, business/finances, and life in general and take control of creation and throw out the outdated paradigms from the past.

Focus on Love and Purpose

You are being shaped and molded to carry out your life, business and mission with greater meaningful purpose. Choose to trust completely and surrender to your journey. Let go of all fear and turn towards loving kindness for all including yourself. Many times in life we check our parachute (fear) so many times we forget to jump (and take action). Sometimes we as leaders, business professionals, moms/dads, friends, co-workers, coaches, and acquaintances fear mediocrity the most - we fear just being average when we are all born to shine and be great. Do not fear being an expert or famous in your field. For you shall remember that the more people you know, the more potential you have to help positively transform lives across your nation and globe. When you begin to live a purpose-filled life, it brings hope and it is hope and love that dissolves fear as fear is simply just love turned upside down. Eventually, you will get to the point in your journey where you recognize that you have fear, however, the fear doesn't have you. When we finally slow down long enough to realize this, it is here we find out what truly matters in life and begin to set our priorities straight, learn how to maintain balance, set clear boundaries and honour our true calling in life with no further agendas attached. When we can finally look ourselves in the mirror and like what we see and can completely let go of our past and all that no longer serves us it is then make the greatest difference.

Another strategy that will help you move forward in all interactions with others including yourself is to remember to always be real and relatable. This can be further defined by possessing the qualities of authenticity, patience, humility, grace, love and compassion that are to be extended continuously or, indefinitely over a longer period of time. What you focus on expands. Be the change you want to see in others. We are all leaders and role models as someone is always watching your every move so make sure you practice what you preach. The old saying goes and couldn't be any closer to the truth "people will not do as you say, rather they will do as you do."

It's imperative to recognize the importance of also staying in balance in our lives. When we are in balance, things in our professional as well as personal existence seem to happen with greater ease than the alternative case of living each moment and each day out of balance. It's extremely difficult to discover consistent expansion, beauty, peace, miraculous encounters, health, connection and pure peace and joy when you're so busy moving through life at top speed just hoping to survive. In order to thrive we need to start paying greater attention how we are showing up in the world. We must fully recognize the direction our life is heading and start making decisions to move towards a place of greater peace, fulfillment, win-win relationships, and purpose. If you feel overwhelmed and as if you are stuck or it is difficult to keep up with your basic everyday tasks, you might suffer from a term that is coined "analysis paralysis." This is simply when we have too many options it complicates our life and feels overwhelming causing us to do absolutely nothing and become completely paralyzed upon taking any action or making a decision one way or another. We need to keep life simple and balanced. Too many choices is overwhelming and leads to stress, imbalance, the innate feeling of being stuck, and a sense of hopelessness and chaos leading to a massive decrease in productivity and company's bottom line over time. I'm sure you can all attest to this concept at some point in your life or another. In fact, a 2010 LexisNexis Survey showed that, on average, employees spend more than half their workdays receiving and managing information rather than using it to do their actual jobs! Did you know there are ***nine key areas of your life that are necessary to focus on maintaining greater balance if you are feeling "stuck"?***

1) Physical: It is important to maintain a healthy physical body through regular exercise, healthy eating and getting enough rest/relaxation and sleep each night.

2) Spirituality: It is important to make sure you take time each day to spend with God in meditation and prayer. Never forget: you are simply a spiritual body having a physical experience not the reverse.

3) Emotional: Honour all of your emotions that surface and know we all experience our feelings on different levels of intensity. It is important to 1) be aware of what your feeling and 2) recognize what's the emotion underneath or root cause of why you are feeling a certain way. For example, the root of anger might be not feeling valued and heard as a child and when similar experiences surface in relationships as adults we become "triggered."

4) Intellectual: Make time to learn something new every day even if it's a "new word of the day."

5) Social: Focus on having a diverse social network focused on human connection from the heart with others and make a regular conscious effort to get to know somebody new.

6) Financial: Did you know that the happiest nations in the world have the least amount of wealth but the greatest sense of

belongingness, community and love? You don't need to be rich to live in abundance.

7) Environmental: Take care of your surroundings including the environment, people, places or things. Declutter your world, focus on positivity and keep life simple. You are in the end, the product of your environment.

8) Relational: This is the ability to relate to others and form deep meaningful connections. The more we can deeply connect with others who are like us and even those not like ourselves, the more you will be blessed with and the greater we will all accomplish together.

9) Mission and Purpose: What drives you to get up in the morning, sets your heart on fire, and is something you would do just because even if you didn't get paid to do it simply because it brings you so much joy and fulfillment? Take bold action on living out your wildest dreams with no regrets.

Balancing all these areas above to the best of your ability will almost instantaneously create greater peace, fulfillment, self-worth and joy. I know when you first think of this, it may seem daunting and even almost impossible, however, I challenge you to take small steps towards creating greater balance in your life each day. This might look like taking a 5-10 minute break to breathe with your eyes closed in between meetings to focus on self-care, or setting clearly pre-defined goals in each category above for the day/week/month to simplify your life, and focus on the priorities in your life that matter most.

We as humans sometimes hold onto the past for far too long. It is through our life that we can learn to step towards forgiveness. If you focus on all the to do lists and "busy-ness" in your life, you may look at this as an underlying way to help cope and ease the deep emotional pain of loss/grief or illness you are feeling underneath. It's simply a distraction to divert you from running from dealing with the ingrained patterns and pains of the past.

Below are a few life lessons I have learned throughout my career that I hope shed light on your current situation and provide hope for a greater tomorrow. Learn to navigate around instead of straight through obstacles in life. When you ask, "why not?" it opens up infinite possibilities. Learning how to effectively and positively react calmly in business and in life to deal with adversaries. Banish indecisiveness and make a proactive choice to move forward. Which path will you choose? Recognize your challenges are your opportunities and change is a part of life. It is imperative to always strive to keep up with what's going on in the world as there has never been a time in history that has undergone a more rapid rate of transformation, growth and infinite expansion as now.

In business we have all gone through disappointments, setbacks, loss and seemingly hopeless circumstances. It is during these times we need to look at our lives and businesses from a greater perspective and become laser focused on the light at the end of the tunnel. We must learn how to detach from the old set points of the past and reset them to maintain balance, integrity, and vitality. Expand beyond to recognize only you have the power to change your set point similar to controlling the remote control to change a TV channel when you are not fond of a particular show. You have the choice at any time to choose to continue to operate on "old channels and patterns" from your past that keep you stuck, or you can dig your heels into the sand and choose to rise above and boldly try a new channel that might even have the potential to provide newfound knowledge that could potentially change your life and business forever. When you stay open to change and unapologetically step into your own power free from the past limitations it is where true freedom is born.

In Summary, take action today and focus on moving towards becoming unstuck. it is up to you and you alone to choose to ferociously walk through the doorway towards the light of whatever version of yourself you wish to be. Make a conscious decision to be united with who you truly are and finally let go of the guilt, hurt, and/or shame. In closing, Abraham Hicks once mentioned that it is time to get ready to get ready to get ready for the big transformation and new beginning and freedom that lies ahead. Make a choice today to do whatever it takes to keep moving forward no matter what simply put because the world needs YOU!

***

To contact Nadene:

www.NadeneJoy.com

Nadene@NadeneJoy.com

Linked In:

http://linkedin.com/in/nadene-joy-227026138

Books:

www.NadeneJoy.com/UncoverYourPurpose

www.NadeneJoy.com/Loveis

Lynette McDonald

Lynette McDonald, CPC, ELI-MP, has been inspiring and motivating individuals, business owners, and professionals since 1990, as a Life Empowerment Coach. Clients have benefited from her instinctual and insightful approach, achieving transformational results. An ordained minister, radio host and teacher at her core, she is a sought-after conference speaker and facilitator.

Lynette believes that within every person are seeds of greatness that have the potential to create a positive impact in the world. It's her life's passion and purpose to inspire, motivate, and challenge her clients to reap the harvest of those seeds. In 2013, she published her first book, *Impregnated with Purpose: Get Ready to P.U.S.H.*

Helping clients PUSH, beginning in 2014 to date, Lynette has ghostwritten or consulted on over 15 books. One was made into a stage play, while another project helped to fulfill the lifelong dream of an original Tuskegee Airman Red Tail Pilot of writing his life story.

No matter which role or office you happen to meet Lynette, it's her desire that your encounter is not just memorable but that you are inspired with promise, infused with power, and ignited with passion.

Can Anyone Really Prosper from Behind B.A.R. s?

By Lynette McDonald

I can imagine that the first thing to come to your mind when you read the title of this chapter may have been of a physical, brick and mortar structure where everyone is dressed uniformly and identified only by numbers. A place where individuals and groups are imprisoned having limited access, resources, and options.

But not all *prisons* are physical. All of us were born into or have inherited various types of prisons formed by culture, race, religion, political, economic, and socio-economic factors. As a result of some experience more than others, the feeling of being locked out from opportunities, or a sense of restricted access to information and resources because of what we believe, as well as the way we respond to those beliefs. This may include how we process the environment around us and circumstances that occur beyond our control. I call these barriers ...***B.A.R.s.*** (**B**elief, **A**ttitude, and **R**easoning.)

It wasn't until around June of 2010 when I received two phone calls that would drastically alter the course of my life. One call revealed the boundaries I was operating in while the other call revealed that I possessed the *keys* to free myself from a limiting belief system and could step out of that mental prison at will. The first call was from my manager with news that I was not expecting. I had been out on medical leave since February 2010, recovering from two surgeries. My role with the organization was of a critical nature, and it never occurred to me that I was "dispensable." So, the news that I was being laid off was a wakeup call.

He went on to explain that the remainder of my expected recovery time would negatively impact service levels, and the position could no longer remain vacant. This was devastating news because my family was already going through a tough period, and we were already feeling the impact of the loss of my income as I was only receiving short-term disability. The worst-case scenarios plagued my mind as I wrestled with the news. I felt stuck. Not the wet, muddy variety of stuck, but the debilitating, limiting, and confining kind. I felt like I was in a prison of my own negative *BARs*.

These included things that I had heard about myself and my life from others that were not supportive. Messages from my past went into battle mode with the then present mission, vision, and plans I had for my life …and the war was on!

It seemed as if every past failure, uncertainty, and fear of what the future might hold for my family and I flooded my mind. I knew if this went unchecked for too long, it would cause frustration rather than motivation to succeed, flourish, and thrive! In other words, I recognized that if I were going to move forward and prosper in the things I was called to do, I was going to have to confront my BARs.

Belief

I understood that I would become the product of my belief system and that I had to tear down the mindset (the mental prison) I had erected. Only I could control how what I perceived as "bad" news would influence the choices I made, which would, in turn, impact the course my life would take.

Attitude

Confrontation with others is generally avoided by most, but I submit that an even greater number of individuals steer clear of self-confrontation. I was faced with looking in the mirror and meeting head-on the prevailing disposition I held towards the matters going on in my life. I had to be honest about my attitude, about the present situation, and of my future.

Reasoning

This is the area where the inherited and learned behaviors can have deep roots. The negative messages I allowed to rest on my mind affected my perception of events and the possible outcomes. My state of mind was the epitome of "worrying about what hadn't happened yet." I had supposed that life as I knew it was over but had based it that opinion on a single event.

For the next several days, I focused on doing the inner work of overcoming my limiting BAR by thinking of empowering and intentional thoughts. I began to tap into my core values and what motivated me to live and work at my best. I reasoned that it was a blessing in disguise to have this fresh start…even if it was packaged as a layoff. My desire was NOT to just get another JOB but to transition into doing what I was born to do.

And that is when I got that life-altering second phone call. The tone of her voice was filled with such excitement and joy, it was almost tangible, and I was immediately transcended mentally and emotionally into the same euphoria. It was as if she were going to burst at the seams if she couldn't get the words out to tell me what happened. She explained that she had some rather drastic changes to happen in her life and, like me, had been seeking direction for her NEXT move. As a result, her journey took her back in time to experiences that included me from nearly 10 years prior. It was based on those encounters that she found her true north. Her wonderful news was that she had just completed a course and earned her certification as a Life Coach. She thanked me for "coaching" her through what she designated as the most challenging events of her life. She went on to explain that if anyone were going to share in her excitement and know the weight of her decision …it would be me.

As she continued to take me on this exhilarating ride down memory lane, I asked permission to interrupt before she got too deep in her story. I had a burning question that needed an answer in order for the rest of the story to make sense. I had to know… *"What is a Life Coach?"* She chuckled and dismissed my question by not dignifying it with an answer. She began again…and then once more… it took the third inquiry to assure her I was quite serious, and my question was sincere. I had not heard of the term *"Life Coach"* before her usage that day. To say the least, she was flabbergasted and, just like a coach, she began to explain to me that "coaching" is what I had done with her over the past 10 years.

As she recounted our partnership, my mind went back in time but not just over the past 10 years with her, but my recollections took me back almost 20 years and included many others. Then it hit me like a ton of bricks…that thing that came naturally for me to do and what I had been doing since the late 1990s had a name. Things like holding individuals accountable to take action to find their own answers to the issues of their lives. Asking empowering questions to help them dig deep to face challenges head-on and having the ability to inspire and motivate others to step outside of limiting boxes... to name a few. Doing what I loved and had a passion for (doing for free) not only had a name, but it had a business model. This was the epitome of the coach, coaching the coach. Her desire to share her story with me planted the seed that launched my coaching business!

As you can see, one conversation sparked an inferno of negative thoughts and corresponding actions, while one new conversation not only put the fire out, it totally healed the mental scarring, and was a balm for my wounded soul. Thanks to an impromptu coaching session, I laid hold of the K.E.Y.s (Knowledge, Expectancy, and Yearning). These KEYS helped me to reach down deep inside myself and access the way out of the prison *BARs* I set up.

Knowledge

From this encounter, I took responsibility for the knowledge I had gained over two decades, helping others. I used this new awareness to deepen my belief in myself and to release my God-given potential and purpose to prosper and succeed using something already in my possession.

Expectation

One definition of expectancy is a mental attitude of confidence and forward-thinking. I set measurable goals and took action to bring my hopes and dreams to fruition. I continued to think prosperous thoughts, and I saw myself and my coaching practice thriving and flourishing.

Yearning

Thanks to "my coach," stirring up the gift inside of me so that I could pay it forward on a grander scale. I was determined not to let anything stand in my way. Soon, the only thing that kept me awake at night was my dreams and having a vision for seeing them fulfilled. I redirected the fuel from the fire that once tried to stop my destiny and blew them towards my passion for helping others.

Today, almost three decades later, I am privileged to still be fanning the flames from that phone call! I get to empower clients to transform negative BARs into revolving doors of unlimited opportunity using KEYs to help them tap into unbridled hope and ignite passions to help thrust them toward the success and prosperity they deserve to realize and fulfill. I get to help clients *break out* of the mental, emotional, financial, political, economic, and socio-economical and other prisons that threaten their prosperity.

As I close out this chapter, I want to share a short story of one of my favorite principles to *Cracking the Rich Code*.

I would love to take credit for such a simple yet profound quote. But I must give credit where credit is due. He was whistling a very lovely, nostalgic tune from the 40's era, and since I've never really met a stranger, I went up to him and asked him if the name of the song he was singing was the classic by the late Lena Horne, "*Stormy Weather*."

After Mr. Irwin introduced himself, we went down memory lane about the song I had accurately recognized. Soon he shared about the person he was waiting for and that he had been invited to share words of wisdom and encouragement at a commencement ceremony. I inquired for a sample of what his audience would hear. Eagerly, in his deep, rich Trinidadian accent, he began to speak with me as if I were his very own granddaughter sitting down on a plush rug near a warm, crackling, fireplace with my knees crossed, and leaning in toward him captivated by every syllable. My intuition signaled to me that I wouldn't want to miss a single word or forget the wisdom he was going to pour. So I pulled out my phone and used a recording application to preserve the message.

Mr. Irwin gave the principal as:

Yesterday is a canceled check

Tomorrow is a promissory note

Today is instant cash…spend it wisely"

Then he gave moral to the quote:

"Yesterday's transactions (our past and our memories) are as canceled checks. They can never be redeposited, changed, or altered, but we can always look back and see the value from what we learned from how we spent them. What does your yesterday say

about how you spent your time, shared your gifts, or worked your plans?

Tomorrow produces hope that we can store up (save for the future – mental messages) as a pledge to ourselves and our loved ones to never give up the pursuit of our goals and dreams. Will my tomorrow reflect the promises you vowed to fulfill?

Today is always "our now" moment. It's the current and flow that drives our currency, which is our motives (mindset.) What are you doing with what is in your hand right now?"

My takeaway from this fortuitous exchange transformed my life and coaching business. It was a gentle, yet powerful confirmation that the KEYs I had laid hold of for both my own life and that of my clients activated the greatness within, to make our mark on the world. My clients are no longer allowing their currency to drop to the ground as if placed in a bag with holes. No longer do they allow BARs to indict, incapacitate, and imprison them but use their KEYs of empowerment to obtain their desired outcome.

Can anyone really prosper from behind B.A.R's?

The answer is an emphatic, "YES!"

***

To contact Lynette:

Website: www.iwpministries.com

Email: iwpministries@gmail.com

Instagram: keawrites

Facebook: Lynette K McDonald and IWP Ministries

Christina Kumar

Christina Kumar is a Google for Entrepreneurs powered 1st place award-winner and the owner of Christina Kumar PR which specializes in placing public figures and businesses in the media for greater coverage. She is also a featured journalist and has interviewed public figures including Russell Simmons, PETA founder and president Ingrid Newkirk, Kate Walsh, and three-time Emmy award-winner Mark Steines among others. Christina has also worked with high-profile public figures in the music industry regarding public relations strategy. Christina is from California and loves collaborating on new projects. She is also a member of the Society of Professional Journalists. If you would like to connect with Christina or receive more information on public relations, visit her website at www.christinakumar.com and sign up to the mailing list.

In it to Win it

By Christina Kumar

You have to be in it to win it. Whatever you do, you have to be all in. There can be blood, sweat, and tears involved but I've realized the more out of my comfort zone I have went to achieve something; the more proud of it I was. I still communicate about moments of time I completely did something successfully bold and courageous even years later. I love having these stories to talk about since they are so fulfilling.

This is exactly what I said when there was doubt during an entrepreneurial competition I had entered. Among the chaos, I said: "You have to be in it to win it!" This gave me the courage to continue on with the competition and to win 1st place with my team. There was doubt, disagreements, and confrontations but because of the "be in it to win it" mindset; I stayed through to the end. Staying power is important when you want to achieve something.

Competition Strategies

Here are a few takeaways from my Google for Entrepreneurs competition win which has given me lessons on how to win in competition and form a business:

The Team Matters: Your team should have complementary skills and be able to get along and communicate well with each other. When there is a gap that needs to be filled, someone should be able to fill that gap.

Good Presentation: Be clear, confident, and well-spoken when you present your idea or service. The more advanced your presentation skills, the better.

Have A Plan: The team should know where they are going and how to get there. There should be clear goals established and they should be followed through.

The end result of our competition was a close call, but our presentation had helped us to win the competition. Since this win, I have met and connected with so many other entrepreneurial-minded people who are both inspiring and talented in their endeavors.

The 4K Plan

Using a strategy like the 4K Plan, which is: Keep Learning, Keep Taking Action, Keep Connecting, and Keep Positive can be beneficial. This strategy can help you by giving you more momentum in your life.

1. Keep Learning

To keep learning is crucial to success. All of the great leaders tend to keep up with the times. Either by reading or joining classes, courses, etc.; this helps gain new and improved skills. Also, with the rapidly changing economy thanks to technology, if you keep up; you will have a chance to excel. It's good to remember the new is constantly replacing the old and if you evolve; you will have a better chance to keep up.

2. Keep Taking Action

Not everyone will be your #1 fan and that is okay. It took one inventor over 3,000 times to help create the lightbulb. If he didn't keep going towards his goal and keep taking action in what he believed could work; would we even have the lightbulb today? Make sure you keep taking action. Progress is important as long as it is helpful and is not only self-seeking.

3. Keep Connecting

You are who you hang out with. It is important to have the right people in your life. By being connected to the right people, doors can open, and opportunities can show up. The best opportunities can show up through a new connection.

4. Keep Positive

A positive mindset helps you to see opportunities. Being grateful helps with maintaining a positive mindset and is a way for you to grow. It is scientifically proven to benefit not only the brain according to studies but also emotions both short and long-term.

Keeping a positive mindset is a key to better relationships and to building new ones.

How are you incorporating the 4K's in your life? Are you leaving an area out? If so, try these strategies based on which of the 4K's you need to start incorporating:

Keep Learning

Workshops: There are many workshops that take place across the U.S. which can be a great learning experience. With a workshop, it's important to have a goal in mind you want to accomplish before you get there. This goal can be as easy as learning something valuable or even networking.

Classes: Continuously learning through taking classes is a great way to learn and can help you be on track to be an expert in your field.

Courses: Now there are numerous companies that provide valuable courses with real-life education you can use to learn about almost any field. Courses can include certifications that show that you have completed their training.

Reading: The top minds of today read at least one book a month. This shows that reading is still as valuable today as it was 100 years ago and is the most convenient way on this list to learn. I recommend a digital book reader since this way you can store and easily carry with you all of the books you need.

Keep Taking Action

Have a to-do list: This can help you to focus more and accomplish tasks that you need to do for the day. This also helps you to organize and remember what you need to do.

Get a calendar: Everyone has had a time where they forgot about a meeting or appointment thinking they would remember it. If it's not written down in a place you will see it; there is a possibility you may forget.

Have a support system: A support system can help keep you accountable. Likewise, the extra support you can gain from having the right support system can really motivate you to do more and give you the courage you need to go further. This is why social networks are so strong; people need to have a community of some sort. There are groups such as the Chamber of Commerce which support local business owners and entrepreneurs across the nation.

Keep Connecting

Attend professional gatherings or mixers: Try to rethink about the next invitation you get to a gathering or mixer; instead of writing it off, go! You could meet your next business partner or business client there.

Accept invitations for lunch or coffee: This can help strengthen bonds with your associates and give you one-on-one time for you to get to know more about them as well as letting them get to know more about you.

Keep Positive

Have gratitude: Have gratitude for what you have now. If possible, keep a gratitude journal. Jim Rohn said it best: "There is no better opportunity to receive more than to be thankful for what you already have. Thanksgiving opens the windows of opportunity for ideas to flow your way."

Respect others: The motto: "Do unto others as you would like done onto you" holds so true in building authentic and strong relationships because, without this mutual respect, relationships aren't the strongest they could be. Also, you never know who someone is connected to.

Have A Cause

As a journalist, I have interviewed a number of high-profile individuals. They are widely known yet still value getting their message across to a newer audience. Not only are they taking time out of their workday for these meetings, but they are also giving valuable advice away. I have learned using your platform for change and awareness is the best thing you can do. Likewise, as a business owner; partnering with organizations geared towards social causes is a great way to give back and add value.

The Value of People

Being able to have spoken to multiple founders of multi-billion-dollar companies mostly in the technology field; I have learned that they have one thing in common. That thing is, being people oriented. Now, it does make sense because at the end of the day, when being an entrepreneur; you have to sell to people and work with people. To do so successfully takes good people skills. Valuing people and their opinions can be crucial to your growth. Being in it to win it means valuing people.

Get A Mentor

A great way to get to where you want to go is by getting a mentor who has already accomplished what you want to do. They should be experienced in the field you want to be in, or you are already in and be a great leader as well. You should also get along well with each other so the relationship can grow easily and be successful. Learning from the best is a good approach to getting where you want to be.

The Right Strategy

Think of a seed. It needs to be planted in the right soil with water and sunshine so that it can then grow properly. Take one of these things away then it won't be at its best or thrive as well as it can. Think about your strategy. Are you using all the keys it needs to create its optimal success? What components is your strategy missing? Sometimes it can only be one to two things that need to be added to this strategy to unlock its full potential. So, what is it? Is it your soil, also known as, your location? If so, take the time to research what moves will work best for you and what has worked for others in the same field.

Asking Is Important

If you want something, sometimes it's important to ask. It's good to step out of your comfort zone to get to where you want to go. I have been impressed by people who have taken a step of faith and received what it is that they've asked for. It sometimes is really that simple. Most people want to help others achieve their goals and if they can; they will. We need to get out of our own way at times and take that next step. By asking for what you want you can gain a better relationship, career, or sales in the fraction of the time it would've taken if you waited.

Having Courage

The best thing you can do is take a stand. I believe that with courage you can do the most amazing things. This is how great companies are made and it starts with one person who took a stand to overcome their insecurities and take the path less traveled; to create a better life for not only themselves but others as well. As an entrepreneur, it takes courage to do what you do as it is not easy but worth it once you see the results. Take Netflix and Amazon; they both were startups that were competing with the biggest companies in their field. They weren't taken seriously at first but in a quick amount of time, they were at the top.

The Right Timing

I had recently spoken with one of the founders of a billion-dollar + company in the technology field. I had asked him, "So how can one know the right timing?" He said, "It's something you practice." We may never know what the right timing is but what I have learned speaking with this tech leader is that; this should not stop you from trying. The more you try, the more you can succeed especially when you are aware of the right timing.

Persistence + Passion Is Key

When you really want something, you tend to have a strong passion for it. This passion can fuel you through the hard times and difficulties to get you through to reach desired results. This is why we need passion in anything that we do. With passion comes persistence. Persistence and passion go hand-in-hand. At the center of any solved problem or great success story, there was passion.

Seek Solutions

The best ideas come from solving a problem. What are some of the solutions that you wish existed right now? Can this make your customer's life easier? If so, you may be onto something. These are some of the useful questions worth asking. It's no wonder why entrepreneurial shows are such a big hit. Everyone loves a good solution. A good solution equals a potentially good business; and if marketed right can achieve great success.

Theme

What is the theme to your life? Do you like it? If not, what is it you need to change? Is it external or internal? Taking a look at these questions is crucial to seeing the realities of your life, and then figuring out the steps to change them. If you love the theme of your life, then good! Most of us will likely be in the middle; happy with some areas and would like to change others. This is when we can purposely seek out solutions to our problems while yet being grateful for our successes. The theme should be gratitude and you can create a new theme. You have that power.

The Right Location

Think of a time where you were in the right place at the right time. What happened? What came out of that experience that changed your life? Have you thought about the experience again after that or did you think it was a coincidence? Either way, being in the right place at the right time can unlock amazing opportunities and putting the chance of opportunity above skepticism can bring positive results.

Creativity

If you were to think about your favorite product right now and then think about how it would have been if it wasn't invented; you most likely wouldn't feel too good about that. The fact that there were people who built a product which most likely had taken a lot of resources, time, effort, and tenacity is a miracle in itself. I am very glad that some of my favorite products; the air conditioner and heater had been created or the winters and summers wouldn't have been as easy to handle as they are now.

There may be people that think there isn't opportunity to create new products because they've all been created already. That's most likely untrue. Most new products are connected to existing products and there's always room for advancement. Otherwise we wouldn't have all the different types of products we have now; we would only have one style of each. Who would want only one choice? As we've seen in the market, there's always room for advancement even if that is a brand-new product or an upgrade of an existing idea; there is opportunity out there and people who are willing to buy it.

Mindset

An in it to win it mindset means that you have to be in the "playing field" to succeed in it. Pursuing what it is that you want and giving it your all. Taking your best shot and going for it without fear. It may be risky, but what isn't? The more you try, the more better you may become. The same with business. You have to be in it to learn and get better. Going in with more experience will eventually give you greater results. It's not always easy and you may not succeed on your first try, but eventually you'll gain a better advantage because of your gained knowledge.

You can become anything you want to be if you are willing and persistent. The more risks you take, the braver you become. You become used to the pressure and as they say; a diamond is created.

If you've been inspired by this chapter, please let me know at info@christinakumar.com.

***

To contact Christina:

www.ChristinaKumar.com

info@ChristinaKumar.com

LinkedIn: www.linkedin.com/in/ChristinaKumar1

Lilia Ackerman

Wellness Coach/ Body, mind, & spirit HCI 2020
Functional Nutrition/Digestive System. Andrea Nakayama 2020
Mastery Life/Health Coach HCI – 2019
TCM/Transformational Coach Method HCI 2019
Health Coach HCI 2018
SIAB/Neuro-Emotional System of Bio-energetic Activation New Millennium School/Miguel MTZ. 2017
Life Coach Wainwright Global Institute 2011
Care for People in Distress. Stephen Ministry 2007
Holistic Practitioner 2003
Healthy Self-Consultant Peggy Krock 1996
Personal Trainer Bally's Nautilus Plus 1993

Transforming Pain to Purpose

By Lilia Ackerman

The Root: It is a proven adage that from our mother's womb we are very aware of what's happening in our surroundings. In a way, it is good to be aware; it is like preparing for our first appearance. The womb acts as a shield of protection that minimizes the intensity of the parents' arguments. I know very well that sense of awareness. I felt my mother's tears of sadness and all the scary commotions around the house. But, even when I was familiar with the loud voices, nothing compared—or prepared me—for the real thing. Without that shield of protection, my sound-proof world evaporated. There I was, feeling helpless in the middle of physical and emotional violence, poverty, religion, and alcoholism.

When my parents decided to go their separate ways, my mom dropped my youngest siblings and me off at her parents' house outside of Mexico City. Overnight, my parents, and older siblings vanished.

The time spent at my grandparents' house helped me connect on a deeper level with life, animals, and nature in general. Both of my grandparents were hard working and loving people. I enjoyed seeing my grandfather feed the horses, watching pigs raising their babies, and laughing when the donkeys were too slow or refused to budge from their pens.

I believe all animals exist on earth to teach us profound life lessons through their personalities—like unconditional love, forgiveness, gratitude, and expressing happiness every time they see us.

I still remember seeing my grandmother, Sara, cooking fresh meals from scratch with so much love and passion. It was inspiring. That childhood experience still guides me today. I have a vegetable and herb garden that I use on a daily basis. Once you taste fresh herbs, you will no longer want things from the market.

One of my grandmother's favorite habits was directing my sister and me to see if the hens laid eggs. She'd put a little basket in our arms and inspired us to collect fresh eggs for our house. She gave me the freedom to run bare foot, play with water, and participate in plays at school. Even though we lived in a small town, the teachers were very creative with the costumes and choreographies.

Life in our village also caused me pain and sadness. One day, I experienced sexual abuse at the hands of a relative who startled me outside the bathroom. I remember sitting on the cement floor crying in fear. After this experience, my voice was silenced and a glass shield was installed between me and the world, creating a loss of communication that lasted decades.

Around Christmas, a beautiful woman showed up with lots of presents for the family. She looked very elegant with her stylish make-up, hairdo, and high heels; she was very different from other women in town. I admired her beauty with tons of curiosity. She acted like she knew me, but I kept my distance from her. Soon I realized—as she was having a conversation with my grandmother—that she was my mother and had come to take us to live with her in a far-away place. I ran and hid behind a door crying. Needless to say, it was very painful to say goodbye to my grandparents.

My mom took my sister and me to Merida Yucatan, where we were under the care of a nanny; she traveled a lot. The new school was far superior to my first one. It was a private Catholic school that required neat attire, clean nails, and combed hair. Every Monday, the nuns measured our skirts to make sure the hems were 10 centimeters below the knee. Girls who broke the rules would encounter the nuns who loved to unstitch the hem all around the skirts. We either laughed or cried that day.

When I turned 9 years old, I was ready to celebrate my First Communion, but I wasn't prepared for another sexual assault. This time, it was the priest who was the catechism teacher. Every week, my mom dropped me off at the church without knowing what was happening there. I felt alone in my journey and it was not a good path. But deep down, I knew it was better to stay quiet. I realized that, when I saw my mom kissing the priest's hand, I knew how important he was for her. So, I followed my instinct and never said anything to anyone about the priest.

Unsettled Emotions: A few years later, my mom stopped traveling and bought a bar situated within walking distance from home. Sometimes, she would let me go with her when she needed my help to conduct inventory. One afternoon, I went on my own because I wanted to tell my mother something that couldn't wait. I snuck in through the back door. Out of curiosity, I looked through the curtains and saw that destiny had another surprise for me. It removed the veil of naivety and revealed a world contrary to the one championed in our society.

I felt unsettled seeing some of my friends' fathers being intimate with women who were not their wives. The strange feeling persisted anytime I saw them when I visited my friends. I felt like they had seen me at the bar that afternoon and realized that I knew their secrets.

Those eye-opening episodes revealed the different and sad aspects of our society. On the one hand, there was the portrait of the perfect, happy family going to the church on Sunday. And on the other hand, there were men who were trying to shatter the ideal family image by having fun with "other" women in bars. And, let's not forget, the priest dressed in long garments, unable to hide the lust of a depraved man.

I saw myself lost in this incomprehensible duality where church and society were orchestrating two parallel realities, besides the emotional conflict I was enduring at home. Before my 10th birthday, I entertained the thought of ending my life. Luckily, my nanny came on time to avoid a misfortune. I was bleeding, but not severe enough to cause irreparable damage.

From this moment onward, my life's blueprint was already established by the acquired experiences—just as atomic particles became part of the cells—creating a world of internal darkness. That meant false beliefs would not allow me to see my path clearly, and therefore, I would live from stumble to stumble, heartache to heartbreak.

Cope with Life: I sought refuge in daydreaming, sports, music, and dance whenever I needed escape from emotional pressure. It played an important role in maintaining balance in my life. I realized that whenever I was stressed, I had a strong desire to run or dance until my body felt at ease and my mind free of pain.

My passion for dancing and my dream of becoming a professional dancer came to an end rather quickly when I had my children. Still, I became an aerobics instructor. This job didn't require any travel and it allowed my body to express emotions that had no rational understanding.

Motherhood: At early edge, I gave birth to a two beautiful souls that changed my life forever. My first child, unfortunately, was born with health-related complications. And after listening to the doctor's depressing diagnosis, I made it my life's mission to give my daughter a normal life, which I did. Her recovery needed different kinds of treatment prescribed by the allopathic doctors. Without realizing it at the time, this mission was the beginning of my journey in the wellness world. I was deeply submerged in the different modalities related to body, mind, and spirit.

A New Start: My marriage was collapsing, and it ended when my husband decided to leave our family and start a new life with someone else. I was lost in the middle of the emotional turmoil, and very depressed. My self-esteem was in the abyss and I couldn't conceive the idea of raising two girls by myself. I had no place to go, no emotional or financial support, so I took the "easy way out" and tried my second and last attempt at suicide.

One night, I asked God to give me a new lease on life and to provide better opportunities for my daughters. I looked at the world map and saw that California was the closest place to Mexico. I knew an old friend there, so I called her and explained my situation. She agreed to let me stay at her place for only 30 days. After taking her up on her offer, I started making a plan, saved some money, and gave away all the little things I had.

Bon-Voyage: In less than six months, I was on my way to California. I took a small suitcase and a box filled with my favorite books. When I was aboard the airplane, I looked at the city lights through the window and realized what was transpiring in my life. I wanted to cry really badly when doubts and fear suddenly ran through the entire body. Then, everything shifted when I reflected on why I was on this new journey. I swallowed my fears and my tears. When they passed through my throat, I felt as if I had eaten a large apple. Somehow, the apple had turned into a heavy rock, and literally, I heard a heavy sound when it hit my stomach. Finally, I was at peace with myself. I put on the airline's headphones and watched a movie.

After arriving in Los Angeles and finding out the cost of the bus fare, I decided to walk everywhere. After walking all over town, my tennis shoes started to fall apart, revealing holes in the sole. I decided to buy a bicycle when I started learning the transportation system. I rode the bicycle around 10 miles a day, from job to job using the water canals as my highways. This kept me in a great shape. Six months later, I went back to Mexico to get my daughters and bring them to California.

My first job as an aerobics instructor was in a small gym. My English was terrible, but not a hindrance when I was teaching the class because the music was very loud and giving cues to my students was just wonderful. After this experience, a new fitness world opened for me, and I found work in many other gyms, like Nautilus Plus, Bally's, L.A. Fitness as a personal trainer and aerobics instructor.

Nautilus Plus was also a school, offering a competitive fitness program; it was authorized to give fitness certifications. As an employee, I received a free education and was able to take as many classes as I wanted. At that time, my English was very limited, so I had to take the same class many times, triggering a recurring question from the manager: "Why do you want to take the class again?" I couldn't tell him it was because I couldn't understand English very well. In my limited spare time, I took every opportunity to educate myself in body, mind, and spirit.

Turning Point: After my second divorce and several broken relationships, I had a deep conversation with God and I asked: "So, what is love?"

The divine appointment of life landed and started revealing itself in a magical way. I realized that it was not about what happened to me that mattered, but about what I could create with my experience living on the dark side for decades. I could use it to brighten this dense and obscure space. My vision was too short just thinking about me when it should have been about others who could benefit from my experience.

I was on fire to seek in every corner of the universe the real meaning of love. Literally, I felt like a shower of light covered me. Imagine a boat sailing in the ocean and about to crash into another ship when it receives the alert signal and is suddenly able to pivot in another direction, saving not only the captain but the passengers' lives too. That's how I felt at that moment.

For the first time in my life, the wires of my brain started to reconnect with the rest of my body, and I heard the alarm before the emotional vehicle crashed. It was the signal to find my purpose, my mission.

In order to clear my mind, I did something unexpected and different, but it was fun. I took a 30-day trip to Europe and North Africa by myself. My family was concerned about me traveling alone, but I assured them that I would be in touch with them constantly. During my first days in Europe, I understood that this trip was meant to be my reconnection with God because we had long conversations about the meaning of love and life in general. The journey started in Madrid, followed by stops in Palma de Mallorca, Portugal, Marrakesh, Morocco, and ending on the Sahara Dessert.

It was a magnificent voyage. It was in Portugal where I realized that my evolving perspective was detailed in a poignant poem that I wrote 10 months before the trip. I recalled that it was about four o'clock in the morning and one line woke me up and wouldn't let me sleep. Finally, I got up, went to the office, and started typing non-stop. One line gave birth to a poem, which was a divine message from god. It was a revelation that I embraced during this trip and for the rest of my life.

My spiritual awakening unfolded like a spiral uncoiled at the speed of light. I learned that I have "a Universal Soul," an expression I'd never heard before. A dear friend introduced me to this concept, which has helped me clarify why people from other countries—like Japan, Philippines, Peru, El Salvador, Vietnam, and India—were speaking to me in their native languages and expecting me to understand them. It was because I embrace all cultures, and I speak heart language, emotions, and feelings.

Once I returned from Europe, it felt like I'd embarked on a new fresh path, a new journey. I was on fire to immerse myself in my inner universe. It was an urge to conquer the unknown. The fear to have an encounter with my inner self evaporated like fog on a sunny day. This action enabled me to hunt the ghosts, beliefs, and pain and emerge into the conscience mind. I broke into tears of childbirth when I saw my inner child trapped in a cell of helplessness, the root of all my emotional issues. I felt exhausted and slept for many hours. But when I woke up, I felt liberated, lighter as if a heavy boulder had fallen off my back.

It wasn't a fun ride, but I understood that I was the one holding myself back, and I was the key to my emotional freedom. At that moment, it was clear what I wanted to experience and what I didn't need in my life.

Life on my Terms: The ripple effect was in full action, knocking down decades of emotional darkness. Healing started to take place in my inner universe. The sour taste of my divorces and many broken relationships found closure and peace. I found my purpose, my mission, and the brightness of my spirituality expanded. My core values and my strengths flourished. My powerful voice rose up again. I had access to a resilient relationship with family, the world, and myself.

Love: The man of my dreams showed up when I least expected it. Today, my reality is to love and share my life with the man who holds my hand even when he is driving, who kisses me for no reason, who watches a silly, funny show with me, and who enjoys a good laugh. Do you want to know more? We have an amazing intimacy. Even when we fight, we argue with passion because our background is Latin and Hispanic. After the fiery argument is extinguished, we end laughing.

To get where we are, our lives have danced to the sound of tango. Sometimes fast, aggressive and distant, sometimes slow, soft and so close that we become one. The more we created room for freedom to express our inner self, accepting our differences and ignoring our mistakes, the more we move in the highest vibration of the Universe: Love.

My Mission: Why does more than 40/50% of marriages end in divorce, and non-married couples last about three years in a relationship? Unfortunately, this is happening because we are emotionally disconnected from ourselves. As a result, we are insensitive to the needs and pain of others, as well as our own. We have to understand that our energy is interconnected worldwide. Consequently, our energies will cross at one point for better or for worse.

Thus, my mission is to reach out to the masses that struggle in their relationships and help them restore their inner selves first. So, they can stand in the authority of love, to be vessels of abundant love that expand over a wider horizon to give and receive love and be more compassionate to others and to themselves.

It is interesting to see how my personal experiences—which were considered my nightmare—became the wheels that put me on the right direction of my life's purpose. They also paved the way to my education in body, mind, and spiritual professions. And that helps me to understand the struggles that men and women may have in finding a meaningful relationship. I know that when we are going through dark moments, we don't recognize the signals that our bodies are communicating before the emotional crash. Until is too late. The outcome is a lonely journey, feeling stuck in an unhealthy lifestyle with chronic heartbreak.

As a Master Coach of Resilient Relationships, I teach men and women who struggle in their love life to transform their own relationships with their inner self first. Essentially, I teach them to first find the extraordinary themselves.

I do this through "The Rolled Method 6 steps to a Resilient Relationship"

Re-Invent The love story with new paradigm and beliefs

Own a resilient identity as their new skin

Let Go of any mental, physical, and spiritual emotional stagnation.

Listen The voice of the struggles, and used their energy to empower your core values, and strengths

Expand To give and receive love

Discover the root of the story and beliefs that have been the whirlwind of your struggles

What is the outcome after working with me?

To be a higher version of themselves

More confident

Stronger self-esteem

More emotionally independent

Have a better control and take responsibilities of their emotions, and actions

Have the ability to cope with problems and setbacks, without falling apart

Be more in-tune with themselves

My coaching style s about a partnership with my clients. We concentrate in crafting their desirable outcome"

Lilia Founder of "The Rolled Method 6 Steps to a Resilient Relationship"

***

To contact Lilia:

(818) 451-7963

E-mail: mylifecoachlily@gmail.com

Website: https://www.liliaackermancoach.com

Facebook: http://fb.me/lilialifemastercoach

https://instagram.com/mylifecoachlily

www.linkedin.com/in/mylifecoachlily

Christine Rose

Christine Rose is passionate about coaching, people, and culture. Her life mission: Compassionately developing people to fully live. Founder and CEO of Christine Rose Coaching & Consulting, a Seattle/Tacoma, Washington coaching firm, Christine helps CEOs and SMEs from startups to $50M annual revenues in a variety of industries to grow leadership, effective and innovative teams, and profitable companies since 2015. Before studying coaching and starting her coaching business, Christine retired from her role as Director of Development at Attain Housing, where she managed consecutive development growth during several leadership changes. A keynote speaker and workshop presenter, Christine is an International Coaching Federation accredited member of the Board of ICF Washington State, certified by Corporate Coach U, a Vistage™ Chair and CEO Coach, a certified Psychological Safety Coach in partnership with The Fearless Organization™, a Taylor Protocols Certified Core Values CVI™ Coach., and a member of Forbes Coaches Council. Her trusted advice and insights are featured on Forbes.com, Public Interest and National Business Radio and internationally on webinars, podcasts and in print. Marshall Goldsmith, Frances Hesselbein, and Sarah McArthur endorsed her Amazon #1 New Release *Life Beyond #MeToo: Creating a Safer World for Our Mothers, Daughters, Sisters & Friends(1/8/2020,)* a coach approach to get to the roots of sexual discrimination and violence, and to create lasting change. Christine earned a B.S. in Business Administration from Georgetown University and Certificate in Fundraising Management from the University of Washington. Christine serves on the boards of Educational Communities Worldwide, Attain Housing, and Urban Business Support.

Sixteen Secrets to True Riches

By Christine Rose

You're not dead yet. Have you had any close calls?

As an infant, during a housefire in the middle of the night, my coughing woke my mother from a sound sleep. Mother smelled smoke, rushed the family outside, and father went to a neighbor's house (before smoke detectors and cellphones) and called the fire department, who extinguished the fire. The next morning, the fire chief told my father, "Your call came just in time. Just a few minutes later, the whole family would have been lost. The flames burning throughout the basement floor, about to breach the door to the main floor, were so hot, the fire would have rapidly engulfed the house, leaving no time to escape. Let's meet tomorrow to design a fire escape plan for your family."

How are your company's emergency plans?

As a teenager, hiking on a steep slope, I slipped off a muddy path. I grabbed the nearest root. Dangling over a 100-foot drop, I saw my life pass before my eyes. Swinging on the root about three feet, I set my toes on a rock, and climbed back onto the path. I made it down alive.

What's your company's root in uncertain times? What's your rock to get you back on the path?

Life may be short, but if you're reading this, it's not over. Age is not a barrier to riches. Soichiro Honda was 42 when he founded Honda Motor Company. Ray Kroc was 52 when he started McDonald's. Harland Sanders started KFC when he was 62 years old. When she was 76, renowned folk artist Anna Mary Robertson "Grandma" Moses created her first painting. As long as you're alive, you can envision your future, make plans, and take actions to achieve your goals.

Secret #1 - We have until our last breath to be rich.

I have no fear of death since I received Jesus as the Lord and Savior of my life. Curious about Jesus? One of the bestselling nonfiction books in history, with more than 35 million copies sold, and more than 70 translations, *The Purpose Driven Life* by Rick Warren is a great resource.

Faith is a personal choice. We are all on a unique journey through life. Stay out of judgment. Be curious about others. Respect people's freedom to believe as they wish. Don't let differences of beliefs keep you from serving customers well.

Secret #2 - Respect others regardless of beliefs.

I've led bible studies, published music celebrating God's kindness, contributed to books and articles, even directed a church retreat. I also taught aerobics and volunteered leading children and adults for over a decade with Girl Scouts, at my children's schools, and at church. Yet twice I wished my life would end. The first time, facing marital conflicts, I saw a counselor. The work reopened deep childhood wounds. The pain was intense. Death beckoned as an escape. I continued working with my counselor, to be there for my daughters and husband.

Even successful entrepreneurs can feel great despair at losses. A couple weeks after Black Friday, 1929, the president of the Rochester Gas and Electric Corporation, who lost more than $1.2 Million (over $18 Million in 2020 dollars), died by suicide by turning on the gas.

If you have suicidal thoughts, reach out. Call your local suicide hotline. In the U.S.A., the *National Suicide Prevention Lifeline* number is 1-800-273-8255. Let go of the lie that it is shameful, or that you are not worth the trouble to let others help you. Take a breath. Life offers a gift of riches beyond monetary value.

Secret #3 –Material wealth without life is worthless. Make a decision today to cherish life and choose your best life ever.

Rich entrepreneurs passionately safeguard their health. Lead your team by example. Adopt a healthy lifestyle. Set limits on work time. Get enough sleep. Nourish your body with healthy food. Avoid depending on alcohol or drugs that numb your brain and slow your progress. Research shows that those who exercise regularly earn up to ten percent more than those who do not. For a richer life, follow a regular exercise program to not only increase your strength, flexibility, and endurance, but to increase the endorphins and serotonin (happy chemicals) in your brain.

Secret #4 – Health is wealth.

Blogging about returning to the marketplace, my thoughts about the comforting promises of God during transition were delivered to an unintended audience. I became a lightning rod for a satanic group whose stalking, gaslighting and sabotage shook my confidence, highlighted my weaknesses, and compromised my safety. If you're seeing inexplicable changes in your environment, or have attracted haters, take action. And take heart. Your success is grounded in the truth. Hold onto your faith. Hold onto hope. Hold onto your love for God, yourself, and others.

Secret #5 - Faith, hope, and love are eternal riches holding divine power for life.

As my daughters finished high school, I transitioned back into to the workforce in midlife, during a recession. Pouring my heart into my work, I had no time for counseling. When the recession halted sales, I took a job as Development Director of a nonprofit, helping homeless families to attain housing and self-sufficiency. I returned to school to earn a graduate Certificate in Fundraising Management. While experiencing an empty nest, unwanted divorce, night school, relocation, and remodel of my new home and life over four and a half years, I managed fund development, marketing and communications, and community outreach, advancing the agency through a merger, two rebrands, team changes, and three supportive executive directors. I didn't let change keep me from performing my best. But self-care was at the bottom of my list.

With so many changes, pressure, and years of gaslighting, depression hit me like a lead brick. I lost the will to live. This time, I pondered how to make death appear accidental. Yet I had a practice of posting on Facebook about things I felt grateful for. One evening, I realized that suicidal thoughts and gratitude are two separate roads, one leading to death, and one to life.

Are you grateful? Write down five things you are grateful for every night. Each morning, before you open your eyes, think of three to five reasons you are grateful. Keep a journal. Search online for free learnings on mindset, meditation, and prayer. Victor Frankl wrote, "The last and greatest of the human freedoms is to choose one's own attitude in any given set of circumstances."

Secret #6 – Choose your attitude. Maintain a practice and mindset of gratitude.

The darkness of the past is history. My boss, with a background in suicide prevention, supported my decision to retire early to get busy living. Family and close friends extended love and faithfulness. A personal trainer helped me recover my health. A counselor helped me do deep inner healing work to secure my foundation. A coach helped me tap into the power of choice to envision and create my best future. We all are surrounded by helpers on our journey. Look for your helpers, and they will appear.

Secret #7 – There is true wealth in your relationships.

Have you made a personal commitment to be a rich business owner? In 2005, with a small income from teaching aerobics to help pay for my kids activities, and little control over household finances, I decided to be rich. At that time, I imagined rich to mean wonderful relationships with family and friends, owning my home outright, paying cash for my cars, working for myself, enjoying life, traveling to new places, and helping one million people live their best life. How would you define rich?

Secret #8 – Decide to be rich. Define rich for yourself.

I was a quiet, agreeable child. Observers noticed nothing unusual. But I carried dark secrets that influenced my internal beliefs for decades. I grew up in a home with three sexual abusers. I was manipulated to maintain the appearance of normalcy, never knowing the next time I would be used. Nowhere to turn for help, I internalized negative, limiting thoughts, which became long held beliefs including:
- I'm nobody, worth nothing.
- There is no help, no safety. It's dangerous to live.
- I'm powerless. There is nothing I can do to get what I want.
- The world is unfair. What's mine will be taken from me.

My freshman year in high school, I spent months soliciting thousands of dollars (USD) in donations from friends and strangers for a March of Dimes walkathon to help prevent birth defects. I walked twenty miles, gathering blisters on my way to a top prize, a new ten-speed bike. I started to believe I could earn what I wanted, through hard work. Weeks later a brother took it out of state to college, left it in the rain, allowed it to rust, and tossed it in the dumpster, reinforcing my old limiting beliefs.

Most people, in spite of solid evidence to the contrary, hold onto limiting beliefs, especially the fear that someone will find them out: They're not good enough to be doing what they're doing. If you have Imposter Syndrome, you may receive accolades in your career or life. Yet no achievement or self-help book you've read has freed you of those unconscious, core beliefs. Have you held onto a nagging fear that someone will discover that you are a nobody?

There are many negative, limiting beliefs. What are yours? Make a list. Then make a list of positive thoughts you'd like to take action on instead of the limiting belief. When you catch yourself with a belief that holds you back, a fear or judgment or old negative thought that no longer applies to your current situation, you can choose to interrupt that thought, and replace it with a new thought and commitment to move you forward in your life.

Imagine holding a party in your brain and inviting to the party only thoughts that will help you live your best life. All of a sudden, negative, limiting thoughts and beliefs come crashing in, and spoil the party! Imagine a superhero that you identify with. Let that superhero be you. Invite that superhero to be the "bouncer at the door of your brain." Tell superhero you that its job is to stop any automatic negative thoughts from gaining unauthorized entry, crashing the party in your brain. A thought may present itself, but you don't have to entertain it. It's your party.

Secret #9 – Release limiting beliefs. Replace them with positive thoughts. Take action.

One key to success in business is to stay curious. Keep learning. Increase your knowledge and mastery of a subject to generate more income. Using what I've learned earning certifications in team Psychological Safety Coaching and Core Values Coaching, I'm able help business owners, leaders, and work teams be more effective and innovative.

I've also explored ways to make life safer for women and girls. During the first four months of stay at home orders during the pandemic, the world saw an exponential increase in domestic violence against women and shocking rise in reports of childhood sexual abuse, primarily against girls. Women comprise a majority of frontline workers with higher risk of exposure to the coronavirus. Women, especially women of color, have borne disproportionate losses through unemployment, reduced wages, and layoffs. Women business owners face greater obstacles in securing credit and government support to withstand the economic downturn. My book, <u>Life Beyond #MeToo: Creating a Safer World for Our Mothers, Daughters, Sisters & Friends</u>, a #1 New Release on Amazon in 2020, shares over a year of learning, along with many stories and life lessons to help business leaders, and societies, create positive change. Find it on Amazon and at <u>www.christinerose.coach/life-beyond-me-too</u>, and stop tolerating gender discrimination in your business and your life.

What are you curious about? What problems would you like to solve? What do you need to learn to help the people you're here to help?

Secret #10 – Be a lifelong learner. Read more books.

Perhaps you've heard, "If you're the smartest person in the room, find a new room." Smart entrepreneurs know they can't know everything and listen carefully to advice of leaders who are smarter and richer. One "new room" for smart leaders is CEO peer advisory groups. I facilitate CEO peer advisory groups where leaders learn from one another. (Visit <u>www.christinerose.coach</u> if you'd like help connecting with other CEOs.) Through coaching and community, CEOs identify blind spots, grow in areas of weakness, get strategic, and accelerate success.

Secret #11 – Connect with smart leaders.

There are countless business mentors in the world to help us keep growing. Many share advice through books. In *Warren is in The Snowball: Warren Buffett and the Business of Life,* by Alice Schroeder, Warren Buffet, founder of Berkshire Hathaway, is quoted as saying:

"When you get to my age, you'll really measure your success in life by how many of the people you want to have love you actually do love you. I know many people who have a lot of money, and they get testimonial dinners and they get hospital wings named after them. But the truth is that nobody in the world loves them. That's the ultimate test of how you have lived your life. The trouble with love is that you can't buy it...You can buy testimonial dinners. But the only way to get love is to be lovable. It's very irritating if you have a lot of money. You'd like to think you could write a check: I'll buy a million dollars' worth of love. But it doesn't work that way. The more you give love away, the more you get."

Secret #12 – Truly rich people know the real measure of success is love.

Jeff Bezos, founder of Amazon, taps into "Day 1" thinking to keep success going. In a letter to employees, Mr. Bezos wrote:

"I've been reminding people that it's Day 1 for a couple of decades...

"Day 2 is stasis. Followed by irrelevance. Followed by excruciating, painful decline. Followed by death. And that is why it is always Day 1....

"To be sure, this kind of decline would happen in extreme slow motion. An established company might harvest Day 2 for decades, but the final result would still come."

Further down the page, Mr. Bezos continues,

"There are many ways to center a business. You can be competitor focused, you can be product focused, you can be technology focused, you can be business model focused, and there are more. But in my view, obsessive customer focus is by far the most protective of Day 1 vitality.

"Why? There are many advantages to a customer-centric approach, but here's the big one: customers are always beautifully, wonderfully dissatisfied, even when they report being happy and business is great. Even when they don't yet know it, customers want something better, and your desire to delight customers will drive you to invent on their behalf."

And, "Staying in Day 1 requires you to experiment patiently, accept failures, plant seeds, protect saplings, and double down when you see customer delight. A customer-obsessed culture best creates the conditions where all of that can happen."

Secret #13 – Obsess over those you serve.

I'm not the only one who thinks relationships and learning are keys to true riches. Bill Gates, founder of Microsoft and the Gates Foundation, reflected in his 2018 year end letter,

"Did I devote enough time to my family? Did I learn enough new things? Did I develop new friendships and deepen old ones? These would have been laughable to me when I was 25, but as I get older, they are much more meaningful." Mr. Gates also advises people to learn from their failures. Contact me if I can help with an assessment and coaching for developing learning safety to accelerate innovation on your teams.

Secret #14 – Failure is a steppingstone to success.

Bernard Arnault, chairman and CEO of LVMH Moët Hennessy – Louis Vuitton SE, LVMH, the world's largest luxury-goods company, became the second wealthiest person in the world in 2019. He is quoted as saying, "Money is just a consequence. I always say to my team, don't worry too much about profitability. If you do your job well, the profitability will come." He also confessed, "I am very competitive. I always want to win."

Secret #15 – Do excellent work. Compete. Be your best.

In 2017, Bezos', Gates' and Buffett's combined wealth exceeded that of half of the United States population combined, over 160 million people. But they cannot take a dime with them when they die. What rich people can carry into eternity is the legacy of the good things they have done for others.

Many people who have a higher net worth would not call me rich. Using Warren Buffett's assessment of success and reviewing my own definition of rich from 2005, I gratefully count myself among successful women with true riches. I have loving relationships, have met many goals, and move towards more. I love helping owners of small to medium sized businesses grow leadership skills, effective and innovative teams, and profits. I help people keep their promises to themselves so they can accelerate progress toward their best future. It's rewarding to celebrate my clients' wins. (You can celebrate more wins by joining my WINS! Accountability Coaching Program, visit http://www.christinerose.coach/group-coaching-for-business-owners/.) And I'm still volunteering on not-for-profit boards and pursuing my goal to help one million people live their best life. True riches, indeed.

How can I help you find true riches? Connect on LinkedIn, Facebook, or Instagram. Let's explore and envision your success.

Secret #16 – Be content, create your legacy by loving and serving others well, and celebrate your wins. You will be truly rich.

Thank you for reading this chapter. How will you take what I shared and use it to move in the direction of your best, rich future? True riches are ahead of you. Now, go get them.

***

To contact Christine:

www.christinerose.coach

https://www.facebook.com/christinerose.coach/

https://www.instagram.com/coachchristinerose/

https://www.linkedin.com/in/coachchristinerose/

https://www.amazon.com/Life-Beyond-MeToo-Creating-Daughters/dp/168314788X

Stacy Oliveri

With a foundation in Art Therapy and a MA in Counseling Psychology and Marriage and Family Therapy Stacy started her work with at risk youth 20 years ago working in a variety of non-profit organizations. But it was her passion and curiosity for the human condition that lead to her own journey of personal growth and transformation. Proving educational experience alone can only take you so far, she discovered the perseverance to turn inwards and heal her own trauma, ultimately became the most important qualification in her work with clients. In 2019 Stacy furthered her education in health coaching and knowledge of entrepreneurship by developing her online coaching practice providing clients with a holistic and creative approach to healing both the mental and physical body.

Zugzwang

By Stacy Oliveri

What kills you makes you stronger. A badass superhuman possessing the good, the bad and the ugly of all those who came before her. Taught only good girls love others no matter what, because self-love was never taught. An ancestral curse that followed her. A burden that required her to dive deep. Outsiders never knowing the enemy lives at home. The situation, the people, the location all changed but one thing stayed the same. Because those on the outside looking in only see what they want to see. But she knows you can't judge the depth of the ocean from the shore. A heart of gold has no value here. It's just shiny, distracting and only complicates everything.

Intuition. A blessing turned on its head. Survival mode is all she knew, a deadly trap of repetitive thoughts. An autobiography written by other people's words. The only thing they asked is why did she stay so long? All I can say is…you know what, forget it, you wouldn't understand. You can only see the truth from your level of consciousness. Not my circus. Not my monkeys. I already am the ringleader of my own shit show. I don't have the time, or the fucks left to explain myself. Besides, the lessons from my past taught me not to trust.

It's a painful reminder. There is an irony in the metaphor. Get a second opinion, they say. I just want to know; do I have Multiple Sclerosis or not? Multiple scarring no one can see but the pain is real. My body is at war with itself. How did I cope? I was thankful it wasn't cancer. Typical and predictable to find the silver lining. I keep trying to convince the world I'm fine because that's what they need me to be. What kind of mother are you? Turning your cell phone off during your final exam. Here's a taste of your own medicine, I will turn off mine so that you will have to call the local hospitals to find out which one your daughters' at. Our daughter, whose hair you used to brush, once upon a time, when I believed in fairy tales, even after the lies. I played the role thinking I was fixing your wrongs. Believing my love could save us all. The father you didn't want to be assuming I was unfaithful because you medically can't have kids.

My tower moment was not one but two. September 11, 2001. To think I made it out alive was so naive. No wonder I took that day so personally. The shame of not remembering the ones brave enough to take fate in their own hands. If the events of that day didn't precede your idea of a romantic getaway, I would have walked the fuck away. What sucks, that if I did, realizing my babies would have not been born.

To heal I had to (I must) purge. How many layers of my lotus flower do I have to peel? How many more tears and snot can I produce? Guess what, divorce doesn't exist. The only freedom from this toxicity is a lobotomy. Still they ask why didn't you just leave? Sometimes I feel like Harley Quinn. An educated therapist love bombed to submission with your crazy. At least the Joker's mask is his real face rather than the coward I see you for. Monsters are real. They exist I know. When I am asked again why I just didn't leave??? My response will be, "because you didn't believe." WTF does that mean requires a level of honesty you are not ready for. I told you already I'm done talking. I refuse to take on anything I am not responsible for. My focus is turned inwards hoping I can still save myself. My life's purpose depends on it. Resistance is the bitch because karma has nothing on me. Broken is the new beauty. My invisible scars protect the most important parts of me. As I chant to myself, "I am not this body. I am not this mind." The violations of both can't even compare to all those who turned a blind eye.

Tell me what's the lesson, the takeaway from the crime. I went from a childhood of molestation by sedation to a marriage of the same demise. Waking up to having sex only to have whispered in my ear, "what are you, dead inside?" There's no time to think, fightback or react. The baby's crying and my MS is in relapse (I think). Our oldest son is named after you, I should have seen the red flags. What's that banging, where's your brother, as I walk up the stairs. Only 4 years old even he sees how life isn't fair. He refuses to talk about what got him so mad. His father views age appropriate responses as pathologies; an attempt to condemn any self-expression. His brother, nearly one year old, his twin sister and mother all have a role. I scream, "I can't take this anymore." No worries she'll be back just like several times before. I'm fed up, overtired, I can't do this anymore. "Here. Hold the baby, I'm done." I checked out, I checked in, taking my shoelaces won't save me. I'm not suicidal. What's the point because I am already dead inside. Silver lining, he doesn't hit me, so why should I leave? When you hear yourself say," If only; It would all be so easy." Careful what you wish for! Didn't see that coming, how could you. Statistically speaking it's known all abuse eventually escalates. I know I am not innocent. I have said my share of mean things; but in my defense gaslighting is a real thing.

The advice I often read is to tell your story. It might help someone else who is struggling or in need. Being silenced over the years has damaged my self-esteem. But there are no coincidences. Just ask the universe and it will be given. If only I believed in the law of attraction. Who knew? I'm a magician. Look what I created. The takeaway from all this; never mind. Forget it. Lesson learned. I can't repeat it. Then along came an opportunity, "are you gonna take it?" How much does it cost? "A small fee of about six thousand dollars with a guarantee of investment." A return of my investment, if only you knew it's twice as much the amount in my checking. The irony keeps coming, the exact amount for selling my ring. Appraised at 25,000, again with jokes, that's just in case states the insurance policy. A robbery, a fire, a flood; possibly all three. That kind of trauma sounds like a cake walk to me. I was groomed since the womb, built to survive but never thrive. Go ahead and try. Wounds have a scent like crumbs leading you straight into the lion's den.

Have you tried mediation? "Yes, it's great, but not now, I'm too busy surviving my fate." What about spirituality, love and light, namaste? My higher self took my inner child to the park today. Does that count? I'm sorry, what did you just say? The dark overlord keeps screaming my name. I'm asked again, why did I stay? I pause and breathe (maybe for the first time today). I consider the magnitude of what I am about to say. Then reply, "did you ever stop to think maybe I did run away? How about asking why I didn't stay away. Pay attention! Here is where this all connects. Trauma is an addiction. Defined by a condition of being addicted to a substance, thing, or activity. A compulsive need for and use of someone or something. Characterized by tolerance and symptoms upon withdrawal. Addictions are not only formed to drugs and alcohol. Addictions in my opinion are the everyday habits that rob us of our time and energy keeping us stuck, to the extent of blocking our own growth and potential.

I wrote the book on how to procrastinate in life. Whether through self-sabotage, avoidance or victimhood I single handedly repeated the lessons life scripted for me. As if being born into a family of trauma and survival wasn't hard enough, I continued to make numerous unhealthy choices from adolescence into adulthood. Never blaming myself for my circumstance but rather searching outward for the answers. My success can be measured by the amount of my student loan debt; huge. Not even a bachelor's degree in Art Therapy with a MA in Counseling was enough to save me from my own demise. Refusing to back down I persevered through an eighteen year emotionally abusive relationship where I was trauma bonded with the father of my children never realizing my real education was obtained from personal experience. Without time restrictions on how long it may take to find myself proved to be my most qualifying attribute as a certified life and health coach.

I understand on a personal level how unresolved trauma literally blocks human potential, abundance and success. As a defense to perceived threat, a coping mechanism, or as self- protection; trauma survivors purposely follow the patterns that retraumatize rather than empower because it's the safer route. The momentum which created the spark in me to shift my perspective was not one but many things over time. It was a process of one step forward and two steps back.

My whole life I have felt like I was in the wrong place at the right time. Love, health and safety is a birthright not a purchase, a goal or a reward for self-sacrifice. True success, true authenticity, true compassion for life is achievable only when you decide to process through inner work instead of going along for the ride. While you sleep, when you shower, when you walk the dog, when you do the dishes. All the mundane everyday moments of this human experience are another opportunity to shift your perspective. Choose. Even in the darkest hour of despair, the choice to evolve or remain always exists. Knowing this changes the game. Even if you are unable to decide in a moment or for a length of time your consciousness is working with you rather than against you. No one can take away your choice to evolve but you, yourself. Let that sink in. There is no pill, possession, or person that can do this for you. Life is a mixed bag of resistance, resilience and reward. You are not alone on this journey, but you alone are responsible for walking the path. There is nothing to sugar coat, no quick fix. Stop worrying about how much time it may take or how impossible it looks from where you are standing. Humility is a virtue that opens doors to unlimited potential. Now is the time to own that shit.

When I was presented with this opportunity as a platform to share my story of success, I was being given the gift to choose. Choose whether the life and circumstances I have always known will continue to hold me back or propel me forward towards my true potential. Monetarily speaking I may be the last person you should be listening to for advice on cracking the rich code. What I will offer my audience is an abundant life is nothing more than choice. Abundance of strength rather than dissatisfaction, of joy rather than lack and lastly a desire to seek meaning and purpose in your life. Choose wisely.

***

To contact Stacy:

www.traumarecoverycoaching.com

traumarecoverycoaching@gmail.com

Aimee Bucher

Aimee Bucher is the Founder & CEO of Harrison Latham Coaching. Harrison Latham is a group of world-class coaches providing unique, powerful programming for organizations that need to increase employee happiness, engagement, retention, and productivity. Harrison Latham has effective out-of-the-box programs but specializes in custom strategies with personalized implementations that bring measurably impactful results.

Aimee is a certified coach through the International Coach Federation. She is also certified in Emotional Intelligence, Predictive Index, Performance Gap Indicator, and Energy Leadership Index. She has worked with a wide range of organizations from single-person startups to established Fortune 500 companies.

Aimee is a classically trained pianist, mother of four amazing kids ages 12-21, and founder of the improv group, #SorryNotSorry.

What Happens When Companies Focus on Employee Happiness?

By Aimee Bucher

I'm going to let you in on a little secret. It doesn't matter what industry you're in, it doesn't matter how big or small your organization, it doesn't matter whether you're a startup or an established company. Focusing on creating employee happiness will have an incredible, positive impact across the width of your organization and from the top all the way down to the bottom line.

If you already know this but are trying to figure out practical ways you can increase employee happiness, jump to the end of this chapter. I've provided a few ideas leaders can begin implementing immediately.

If you're wondering why happiness matters in business, keep reading; it's a wild ride.

So, what actually happens when a company focuses on employee happiness? Why does happiness matter in business? You might be surprised.

When a company has happy employees:

Task accuracy improves by 19%[1]

Productivity goes up 20%[2]

Sales increase 37%[3]

Given these statistics, the question should become: Why don't more companies focus on employee happiness? What could your company do with 20% improved productivity or a 37% increase in sales?

A NOTE: This book is being published as we are in the midst of a global pandemic and you might be wondering why we're talking about happiness when there are really pressing issues around operations and cash flow. COVID-19 is changing our understanding of ourselves, our world, and our connection with one another. This pandemic is essentially giving us a global crash course on just how connected we are as humans.

Our humanness and our happiness are intimately intertwined. Coping with uncertainty at a global level is completely new and many people are struggling to find their grounding. Brands will be judged — some quite harshly — by their employee treatment during this time. This is exactly the right time to talk about our collective happiness and how to increase it.

I'm going to give you practical ways for your business to increase employee happiness, but first, let's make sure we are in agreement about the meaning of "happiness". Defining happiness is trickier than it might seem on the surface. Simply talking about happiness tends to bring out a wide variety of opinions, some very strongly held, about what it truly means to be happy.

There is a huge range of understanding about what happiness actually is and how we experience it. If you survey people asking, "How do you define happiness?" you'll get all sorts of answers. Some people say happiness is a fleeting emotion and pursuing happiness itself is detrimental. Others argue that happiness only comes from serving others or going outside of one's own wants and needs.

Even researchers don't agree on a single definition of happiness. Some say it's an emotion, some say it's a feeling, some say it's a created state.

I define happiness this way:

Happiness is a deep soul joy born from full acceptance of one's humanness and belief that life has purpose and meaning.

What does happiness look like in an organizational setting? How can a company focus on helping their employees create a "deep soul joy"?

Think about a typical Monday morning in any business you've ever worked in. What was it like as people walked in the door? What was the overall mood? In general, how happy were the employees? Do you have that picture in your head?

Now, imagine walking into work on a Monday morning and every person — including you — is genuinely happy to be there. How would productivity be different? What would change about how the teams communicate? What would engagement levels look like?

As a culture, we just assume that work is going to suck for most people. Work is work. It's not supposed to be enjoyable. This is why we spend so much time talking about work-life balance.

Life is good. Work is not.

Does that really have to be the case, though? Why can't work be good or even great? Why can't we adjust our company cultures to create happiness in the lives of everyone there?

Happiness is crucial to how we view the world, how we work, and how we cope with challenges. Increasing our collective happiness is one of the most important things we can do, especially right now. And there's no better place to start than at the top.

You might think workplace happiness seems unattainable and idealistic. You might be thinking, "Seriously, have you met the people I work with?!"

You're a leader. It's well within your power to create a company culture that supports and creates happiness for everyone who works for you.

And here's the thing, focusing on happiness in ways that make a difference is not actually that difficult and the benefits are incredible. Increasing happiness creates ripples in the lives of your employees and customers that have far-reaching effects. Changing the happiness levels in your organization will affect more lives than you can imagine.

Focusing on happiness will also move you further out in front of your competitors and increase your bottom line. You just have to make the conscious decision that happiness matters in your organization and then put in the effort at all levels of your leadership.

There are many things you can do to increase your employees' happiness. Here are three simple and practical things you can implement immediately to create more happiness in your organization.

1. Express Gratitude

It is commonly said that if you want to be happy, be grateful. Basically, expressing gratitude shifts your perspective to find the more positive aspects in any situation. And, gratefulness is like a muscle; the more you use it, the stronger it gets. When you are intentionally looking for things to be grateful for, you'll find it easier and easier to find things to be grateful for.

Express gratitude to your employees and customers. Be specific and generous with your gratitude. Start meetings with gratitude. Challenge your employees to do the same. Ask your people what they are grateful for and push them to give you meaningful answers.

Searching for things to be grateful for will literally rewire your brain. You'll find yourself happier and more positive in general. You increase your happiness when you savor the moments, the people, and the things in front of you.

Exercising your gratitude muscle also provides a boost to your mental toughness and resilience.

A few years back, I did a personal challenge for myself. I decided it was my "Year of Gratefulness" and I posted one thing I was grateful for everyday on social media. That simple act of posting my gratefulness every day was literally life changing. Halfway through that year I got divorced and then fired from my job. Those are pretty big life events and they came within seven days of each other.

But I had been working on my gratefulness muscle and it was pretty strong by that point. Instead of seeing all the drawbacks in those hard situations, my brain immediately focused on what I could be grateful for. I realized I was genuinely happy and excited to have a chance to re-start everything in my life! Had I not been practicing gratefulness for the previous six months I suspect my reaction would have been different.

2. Provide Time Abundance

Time abundance is the new rich. Feeling like we have free time or even just enough time to get everything done is one of the keys to feeling satisfied with life.

Sometimes a team or an entire company can be under a deadline and time abundance simply isn't possible. But, if that's the regular expectation, you'll have unhappy, burned-out employees with a high turnover rate and that's going to cost your organization a lot of money in the long run.

The fact of the matter is we are not our best selves when we are time stressed. There is a famous 1973 study by Barley & Datson4 where seminary students were presented with a staged "Good Samaritan" scenario. The students were told they needed to give a talk about the Good Samaritan story, and they were told they were either late and had to hurry or they had plenty of time to get to the place where they would be speaking.

On their way, the students encountered a man slumped in a doorway who coughed and moaned as they approached. The researchers found only 10% of the students in the "hurry" group stopped to help as opposed to 63% of the "plenty of time" group.

When we feel like we don't have enough time, we are much less likely to act in accordance with our values. That group of seminary students who didn't stop to help felt terrible about not stopping to help. It wasn't that they didn't care; they felt like they didn't have the time.

Your employees want to do their best work. They care about their work, but when they feel time stressed, they're not going to be their best selves. They're going to simply "get the job done" but not necessarily to the best of their abilities. Remember the stat at the beginning of this chapter: happy employees are 19% more accurate at their tasks. Having time abundance is directly related.

3. Power Lead Your Conversations

Starting your conversations with something powerful and meaningful can change the entire dynamic of conversations for the better.

For example, you see a colleague and they ask how your day is going. You can respond something like this; *"I've had back to back meetings all day and I'm worn out. I'm looking forward to some time away."*

OR you might say, *"I've had back to back meetings all day and I'm tired, but excited about the new things being implemented."*

Notice the difference? Even just reading those two statements feels different, doesn't it? Starting conversations with something powerful and meaningful shifts the tone of the entire conversation. As a leader, you can shape conversations. It doesn't mean you don't discuss negative things or challenges, but the way you frame those challenges with your words and attitude can make all the difference for you and your employees.

If you haven't started conversations this way before, it will take a conscious effort to remember to do so. Challenge yourself to do it for a day or two. You might be amazed at what you learn about yourself and how conversations open up in whole new ways!

These are just three simple ways you can increase happiness in your organization. There are plenty more, but until happiness is woven into the company's cultural fabric, these tactics won't necessarily have lasting impacts.

The anonymous app, Blind did a survey of 3.2 million people about their workplaces and Netflix ranked as the company with the happiest employees. Do a quick online search for "Netflix Culture Deck" Or visit this link: jobs.netflix.com/culture and read the guide to Netflix company culture. This guide is a case study in how to clearly define company culture in ways that include happiness as a core value.

Your people are your greatest assets. Without your people, your organization doesn't exist. Creating a long-term strategy for building a happiness culture is one of the most important things you can do for your company. When you have happy employees, you can withstand market downturns, bad product releases, and even global pandemics. When you have happy employees, you see increased productivity, greater retention, and more sales. Happy employees will support and drive your vision for your organization.

So, how happy are your employees? And what are your next steps to create a culture of happiness?

---

[1] https://hbr.org/2011/06/the-happiness-dividend

[2] http://www.smf.co.uk/wp-content/uploads/2015/10/Social-Market-Foundation-Publication-Briefing-CAGE-4-Are-happy-workers-more-productive-281015.pdf#page=9

[3] https://hbr.org/2011/06/the-happiness-dividend

[4] http://faculty.babson.edu/krollag/org_site/soc_psych/darley_samarit.html

---

***

To Contact Aimee:

419-234-6971

linkedin/in/aimeebucher

harrisonlatham.com

aimeebucher.com

Marcus Anthony Ray

British born in 1962 he came to Canada in 1965

At 9 Marcus hit the stage as a **singer/guitar player**

At age 15 he was recruited as a **male model**

In the financial crash of the early 80s he reluctantly entered the world of **male exotic dancing**

After 7 years of dancing he invested in his own **Agency** for male strippers.

After selling to the competition Marcus invested in **Night Clubs.** All of the above he had achieved before his 30th birthday.

He then sold everything to become a **Police Officer** and **Search and Rescue Diver.**

After serving 6 years he felt the pull of his entrepreneurial spirit and decided to attend the **London School of Hair Dressing** in hopes of opening a **Salon Franchise.** Drawing designs for the salon he created unique furniture pieces. People began ordering the Custom Vanities and before he knew it Marcus launched the **PEBBLECREEK Furniture Company**

After years of success, his own factory, 10 store locations and a **Construction Company** all was lost due to an economical crash.

Now at 58 Marcus is an **International Award-Winning Speaker** and **Author**

Cash in Your Failures for Success

By Marcus Anthony Ray

Adversity! Now there's a word I'm familiar with. As a lifetime entrepreneur the road has never been an easy one. To be absolutely truthful it's felt like climbing a cliff with an extra 200 pounds of shit strapped to my back, only to realize once I clawed my way to the top there's another cliff to climb, and the damn things steeper!

I've always been that guy with the ideas, you know, the one that thinks everything up and then tries to get everyone else to believe in it. Only to have them all jump on the band wagon and push me off!

But hey, I'm not trying to sound negative here, I've actually had an amazing life filled with many different careers. I was the lead singer in a rock band, and I got to tour with some of the great bands of the 60s and 70s. It was an amazing time in my life. But wait, before you picture me as some aging rock star with frizzy grey hair, and skin like raw hide, let me clarify. I was only 12 to 15 years old at the time. This was truly my first taste of success, and my first experience of all the ups and downs that came along with it. I had fans, I gave out autographs, and I made lots of money! It didn't take me long to be the only 17-year-old in high school with a brand new Corvette. I remember thinking to myself "is life always going to be this easy?" However, as time went by, my interest in my music career diminished. Being a member of a young rock group became tiresome, as all we did day in and day out was practice with the same group of guys. It didn't take long before playing became a chore rather than a pleasure. Before long, each and every one of us went our own separate ways.

I entered into the world of male modeling at the ripe old age of 18. Seeing as modelling was mainly night work, I filled my days working as a carpenter. I thought I was doing well, but what came next at 20 years old was never part of the plan.

For those unfamiliar with the early 80s, the interest rates skyrocketed, and the housing market plummeted. A number of family members, including myself and my father, lost our jobs. This event would add a chapter in my life that I would only later recognize as incredibly significant. I had been working out in the gym bodybuilding for some time, and without knowing it I had every asset needed to move into my next line of work. Soon after getting into modeling, I became a male exotic dancer. That's right, you heard it correctly. I did say male exotic dancer. When I began dancing my goal was simple: pay the mortgage on the family home so we wouldn't lose it. Getting into it, I had no idea that when the music played, the women screamed, and when I wiggled what I had, that in time I would get completely hooked. The money, the female attention, and the partying were alluring. At the height of my career I became Mr. Nude North America, and what was the value of that? Let me just say this, I made unspeakable amounts of money for the 15 minutes of entertainment I provided per night. That dark intoxicating world of male stripping had drawn me in, altering my sense of reality, and moral standing.

Was I successful? Hell yeah, I was successful. I was at the top of my game and was named one of the top male exotic dancers in the country. Financially, it's the most money that I've ever made in such a short period of time in my entire life. Despite the money, my success would also become the first of many in a long line of failures. Sex, drugs, and alcohol took its toll on every aspect of my life. It became a matter of quit or die - by the way, it's ok to quit doing something if it's trying to kill you. It took a death-defying car accident to bring me to my senses. But thank god, and the guy who pulled me from the burning twisted wreck, it certainly didn't end there. My life would take many more turns, both good and bad, before I discovered success's deep secrets.

After surviving the crash, beating every addiction I had cold turkey, and leaving the stage, I opened my own agency to represent other top male exotic dancers. There was no stopping me, in fact, there never has been a way of stopping me from pursuing success. When an opportunity arose that I couldn't resist, I sold my agency and began buying night clubs - a very lucrative business. Once again, I found success, but before long I also found failure as well. The club across the street forced me into a drink war. Prices dropped along with the profits, and I could tell the end was near. I've always had the right idea at the right time, but I've lacked the discipline and the staying power to hold it together. It was time to reinvent myself, time for a complete change, and time to do something completely out of the ordinary.

I became a police officer with the Royal Canadian mounted police. Now that's what I call reinventing yourself. There's no doubt joining law enforcement definitely helped shape the man that I am now. Though my time with the police force was only six years, the insight from my experiences was the most priceless compensation. I'd found the one thing that I had lacked all those opportunities ago: discipline.

Upon leaving the police force, I launched one of the largest furniture manufacturers in British Columbia, Canada. I grew from a 400 square-foot garage to a 25,000 square-foot factory and 10 of my own retail stores. Now you're probably thinking… here it is, this is what he's going to talk about: his biggest success. Well, without a word of a lie, this was the biggest success of my life. Get ready, because here comes the "but!"

Staying true to being transparent, I can't tell a lie. The furniture company was also the biggest failure of my life. Why? I was over leveraged in 2008. Through no real fault of my own - which is what I prefer to believe - I found myself in trouble once again. I have always been a firm believer that every experience we have, no matter the cost, we gain something in return. Whether that something be good, bad, or ugly, we walk away with some new knowledge. I've learned more from my failures than I have from my successes. Each time I rose, then fell, I gained! In fact, after each devastating failure, I rose higher than the time before. I don't quit! Okay, except for the stripping thing, but who's ever heard of a 65-year-old stripper? That career was going nowhere…fast!

You've probably heard the term quitters never win, and winners never quit! These aren't just words, it's a point of reference. No one runs half a race and is declared a winner, no matter how hard it is you have to give it everything you've got till you reach the finish line. Being an entrepreneur is no different. I've always known this, which is why I've never quit, I've never thrown in the towel, and I have never stopped pursuing what this book refers to as the Rich code.

My success now is the result of all my failures. I have taken the story of every financial demise in my life and shared it with audiences from around the world. Everything that should've been my end has always become a new beginning. From my varied experiences, and countless times reinventing myself, I have created enough content to become an international award-winning public speaker. A public speaker you're thinking?

Now, I've got you thinking that I'm some kind of Guru travelling the world telling people how to be successful and live better lives. In a sense that's true, it is what I I'm doing, but please allow me to toot my own horn - I was getting extremely successful at it. I toured the USA being a featured speaker with Mark Yuziak from Las Vegas. I was on top baby. Nothing can stop me now I thought. I was in New York city where I had just been filmed on a TV show about my book when the problem hit - COVID 19! Talk about having the rug pulled out from under you!

No more crowds to speak to, no more interviews, no more of my programs being sold. It had all come to a complete stop. I flew home from the USA back to Canada in complete disbelief. How is this even possible that entire countries would shut down? That people would not leave their homes? that businesses would close without even knowing if they were opening again? In that moment fear ruled the world. I mean come on, is this shit really happening? A global pandemic. Really?

Let's be honest here, I can handle adversity, but this was rapidly becoming the biggest challenge of my life. For the first time in my life I felt devastation, I felt depression, I felt pissed off, and quite honestly, I contemplated quitting. This wasn't just an economic crash. The governments of the world closed down business, they disallowed our daily routines, and they ordered people to stay in their homes. They essentially ordered the population of the entire world to stop living. Then it began: conspiracy theories ran rampant, depression, suicide, crime, and domestic disputes all seemed to increase over night.

Replacing human contact, everyone turned to the Internet to communicate instead. Those who were public speakers, mentors, and motivators all went online to get their message out. The Internet was flooded with how to do this, how to do that, how to survive this latest crisis. The more I thought about things, the more I needed to do something different. Just to go online and tell people to keep their chins up seemed quite futile. Just when the moment seemed at its darkest, I thought to myself, what can you give to people who've had all they know taken away in one fell swoop? They are now in a position where they don't know who to turn to, they don't know who to believe, and they don't know where to go. I ask you, what do you say to those people? That's when my creative juices begin to flow. Here's what I thought: give them a place to go!

The answer was right there in front of my face, not a simple answer, but it was the right answer. At a time when many people felt unsafe to be in this world. My partner and I stood up and decided to give them a new place to call home, and a new place to feel safe!

We have created Riverdell Adventures located in the kettle valley of the Okanagan territory in British Columbia. Opportunity was knocking at the door. No one was out and about, no one was looking at land, and no one was looking to purchase anything. Can you think of a better time to go out and buy something? We found the land and now we are building Riverdell. An RV park with cabins, a recreation center, and all the amenities you can dream of. A place where people can go and not only feel safe but feel free.

You see true entrepreneurs keep their eyes open and stay alert. Opportunities are popping up 365 days a year but the ones that see it are those who understand the Rich Code. I'm sure you're saying to yourself okay, this sounds like it's great idea if you have the money. Well, because of COVID-19, many people did not want to stay in the stock market any longer with the world seeming so uncertain. Therefore, investors are ready and willing to step up. You, who's reading this book now, have purchased it because you feel the answers are within. If you pay attention to all that's written within these pages, you will discover the code to truly being rich and feeling fulfilment within your lifetime.

Whether I succeed at this ripe age of 58 years old or I fail, I know that my failures are not my end. They are the beginning of the next stage. With this way of thinking I have become fearless. I am willing to take whatever risk may fall upon me to reach my goal. We are all capable of realizing the dream. Full commitment and determination, taking your passion and turning it into a burning obsession is the secret. I realize that as you read this for the first time, it may just seem like words coming from someone you don't know, and someone who's had experiences far different than your own. Well I'm here to tell you all experiences, no matter how small, are important when combined with the direction in which you're going. Do you have a destination in mind? Is there a goal you wish to achieve? Are you like the rest of us and hopelessly searching for happiness and financial freedom? Well of course you must be, why else have you bought this book? Why else have you read each story and taken in the passion that leaps from the pages? Every writer has taken their own unique journey that brought them to where they are now. Every writer here is giving you the clues to reach your own personalized version of success. We are all unique in our own way. We all dream. To reach those dreams you need the power of the mind body and soul. You take all your positive energy and focus it on one path and one path only. See the finish line and run your own race. Success belongs to everyone, happiness belongs to everyone, and financial freedom is the result of relentless effort put out by those who refuse to quit. For those who believe, not only in themselves, but in the rewards given to those who try, absolute success is inevitable! I found that belief was my strongest asset. In everything I tried I believed I could succeed, and in each effort given, I did succeed. For all the times I failed, there was an invaluable lesson to be learned. Think of that lesson like it's cash to be used to purchase your next success.

Take a moment to look back, see what you have learned, ask yourself, "How can I use this for my next venture?" Experience becomes knowledge, and knowledge has a value that can be leveraged in the pursuit of success.

From my young rock star days, I gained courage. Playing and singing in front of thousands of people at such an early age. From being a male exotic dancer, I gained confidence. Placed in what I would think to be one of the most vulnerable positions of my life, I showed up and I kicked ass!

As far as my first big failure, I stood up, brushed the humiliation off my ego, and gained the power of fearlessness.

Regardless of whether or not I failed or succeeded in what I did, I always treated each new experience as a learning opportunity. All that I have done or been is now who I am! I am courageous, confident, fearless, and I possess a vast knowledge of what the human entrepreneurial spirit is capable of.

Now if you believe that I am everything I say I am. Then the next little piece of information I share with you just may be what you've been waiting to here. I will tell you my secret. The secret I'm speaking of is how I, Marcus Anthony Ray, have *cracked the rich code.*

I simply believed heart and sole that my DREAMS WERE REALITY WAITING TO HAPPEN.

…….and so are yours!

YOU ONLY FAIL WHEN YOU LOSE THE WILL TO SUCCEED.

Marcus Anthony Ray

***

To contact Marcus:

www.marcusraytalks.com

Monica Griffin

Hi! I'm Monica Griffin. My friends and family call me Mo. I lost my father when I was 11 years old. It wasn't an easy transition. By the time I was 18, I had lost six friends and experienced traumatic car accidents; 5 of my friends were in one horrific accident. Since the time I was 17, I knew I wanted to change the world; I just didn't know how, or even if I could.

Three years ago, I was introduced to life coach certification where I was able to utilize all of my life experiences, traumas, and griefs; I was finally able to use my experience being a survivor of rape and sex trafficking, to help others presently with their own lives. Becoming a life coach was my dream come true, even before I understood what this title meant.

Now at 30 years old, not only do I have my own brand called Mo Life, I'm also a partner with a holistic medical clinic that specializes in integrated medicine. Mo Life is going to be more than a brand. It will be a movement to teach others how to genuinely love, understand, and appreciate themselves in their environment. I'm so proud of what Mo Life has become, and am even more excited to know there is much more to grow and succeed in.

More to Life

By Monica E. Griffin

You must believe in yourself to be the best version of You possible. That is the first step to a healthy mindset. Along with being the best version of yourself, comes an open mindedness that accepts criticism to help you grow and succeed and stop looking at obstacles as obstacles; Embrace those obstacles, look at them as challenges. Look at obstacles as a lion sees its prey. Take charge, run after them, pounce on them…even rip them to shreds and show the challenge what you are made of!

I believe, because of this mindset, elevating yourself to the rich status you desire is more than just a strategy. Constantly finding myself pushing limitations and thinking outside of the box, and never allowing the word, 'No' to get in the way of my end goal is my way of being a lioness in the world we live in. To get to the top, a person will sometimes be labeled as 'Rebellious,' 'Selfish,' or even 'Careless.' These labels are misleading to the untrained ear; they are statements we should perceive as empowerment.

When you think of a rebellious individual, what comes to mind? Maybe that they do things differently than they are told to? Or possibly those people take the road less traveled because they do not want to be told what choice to make? Being a rebel to me means I do not go by the code or rules that are applied by the textbooks. This nature is more along the lines of thinking, "There is more than one way to skin a cat."

Many people make the mistake of thinking selfish individuals are only concerned about themselves. That is inaccurate. Selfish people know what they want and have a plan of how to achieve it. This does not mean they step on others to get what they desire, need, or choose. These people can recognize what brings happiness to their lives and what does not. In my experience, these people are the ones who see a vision of success clearer than that of their peers.

Acts of carelessness are mostly seen negatively, like hurting another being in some way, shape, or form. Carelessness without being kind is when humans get themselves into situations that make them seem like the bad guy. If you cancel plans because you simply see a better opportunity to thrive in a different situation than the one you have committed to, is not an act of not caring; the reality of the situation is you are bettering your chances of becoming successful. When you feel there is a better opportunity knocking at the door, open it! Even if it means closing the original door. Though, when those commitments are broken the other party may feel as if you really did not give a damn to begin with, and it is OKAY. Perception is everything in life. Be kind, let the other party down gently, then while hanging up the phone, or walking away from the seat you were about to sit down in for the meeting, roar like the animal you truly are in your heart, knowing you have made the best decision for you.

I'm Monica Griffin, but you can call me Mo. MoLife is my life coach company that is setting new standards for all life coaches. We are ever changing and ever evolving in our realities and within our personal identity. We are constantly finding our purpose in life whether at home, at work or even when we are out with friends; we are constantly driving ourselves. Well, I say F**K THAT! Why do we push, why do we set such high expectations for ourselves without ever focusing on the NOW, the Present Day? Why do we always put ourselves in a box and expect everyone around us to notice us in the box? Why not Be the Unexpected? Why not be the Thinker Outside the Box? Why not just simply be YOU without the labels, titles, degrees, certificates, and resume? We do not need those to define who we are, they simply help make our identities sparkle. Why not build on your knowledge, experiences, and life's hard challenges to be your true identity? This is when I, come into your reality and create the reality that is custom fit to YOU. What makes YOU tick? What are your triggers? What was your childhood like? Where does your anxiety, depression, stress linger from? How can I help you be the most captivating version of yourself? How can I help create your reality with the healthiest mindset you have ever had?

It is all about YOU! Allow yourself to give in to a little ME time! Time to take charge of your reality, let go of the chains that have been holding you down, let go of guilt, let go of who you think you are and BE who you KNOW you are! There are versions of you that no longer exist in this world, and people want to believe they still know you. Let us prove them wrong. We get one shot in life to make the most of every Present Day, so why not be the superhero of your own story?! F**k the past and let us begin to create our brightest present and future. You need me as much as you need to shout from the cliffs, "F**K IT, I AM ME!"

MoLife came to be because of a traumatic accident that happened in my hometown in 2008; 5 of my friends were killed in the same car accident that shook our little town to the core. This life changing event showed me that my compassion for my friends and community was much stronger than I ever knew. I offered a listening ear and a shoulder to cry on for many of my friends and classmates. From the time I was 17 years old, I wanted to be someone who listened and helped others succeed. Even in high school I was a problem solver, not just for my friends, but for my school, at part time jobs, and even with my hobbies.

What makes MoLife life coaching different from others? Though many life coaches view themselves to be custom fit, most follow a general script to your problems. MoLife coaching is different because there hasn't been a script written for the demographic that MoLife specializes in. This means that each client has their own unique, customized experience, which allows me to give you one-on-one attention. There is no script or quick solution to the scars our past has left on our hearts. The millennial generation is newer territory for life coaching, which gives MoLife the creative, customized experience that isn't offered by other life coaches.

Each session with me is between an hour to two hours long. I have the ability to have a session with you via phone call, face-to-face, or Facetime. I want to accommodate you during this session. We will discuss in great detail your past, and I will challenge you to dig deep. Tell me how you feel, why does this make you feel this way...cry, scream, cuss, tell me everything you should have been allowed to feel 10 years ago (give or take)! The purpose of this is to make you feel. Many people are numb to their lives. I want you to feel. Feel...like you're supposed to...be an extraordinary human instead of a walking numb individual on this earth. Because You matter, and You have a purpose!

After each session is complete, I will email you brain coaching exercises. I will ask that these are completed by the next session where we will spend time going over them, and once again, digging deep. We will continue where we left off from our previous session, and I will make changes to our exercises as I see fit for you to graduate my program and become the best version of yourself!

My program is all about you and is extremely flexible. Life is full of ups and downs, and sometimes (a lot of the time really), things do not go the way we plan. One of my greatest strengths is that I am extremely adaptable. If my program needs to be altered in a way that better suits you or your lifestyle, I am up for the challenge! I am here to help you. I live for it, it awakens me on the inside, and that's why I chose it as my profession!

My secret is that every step, twist, turn, and impediment brought me to this "ah ha" moment 3 years ago, when a local California life coach introduced herself to me. She asked if I was the local influencer that worked with the non-profits in my small surf town community. I was shocked to have such a title because I only thought of myself as a community advocate and entrepreneur, helping others follow through with their goals. I never thought I was changing lives as my own mindset was on one person's goal at a time. This was such a pivot point in my career. I took a certification course and recognized this was what I had been working toward my whole adult life. Every avenue brought me to this moment of becoming a life coach, an Influencer. So, how am I changing the standards of life coaching?

I am 30 years old and a business partner with a holistic medical practice where we specialize in IV infusion therapies and brain coaching. I did not get here overnight, nor did I flirt my way to the top. I got here because of my charisma, because I fought to see the light at the end of the tunnel, which made me the life coach I am today. My technique is a simple plan of action. I shake hands and network every day, whether on social media platforms or in person through community events and volunteering for non-profits in my town. You see, all the actions you take to be successful will mirror your success. So, if you see yourself being an influencer/thought leader with a loud voice, it all starts with your community. It all starts with how you volunteer. It all begins with how you present yourself and how you impress others by the way you hold yourself. There is not rocket science behind how we can crack the rich code, but every strategy needs a blueprint. Every blueprint needs paper and pen and every pen needs ink.

So, just like your strategy on paper, you need to mirror your vision with the best version of you and give yourself the illusion that you are on top even before you get there. But promise me this, when you get to the top, you will continue to climb! No true successful entrepreneur will tell you that they have met their goal, and if they do, let that be a warning that they no longer believe in their true potential. No entrepreneur that hungers for more will tell you that they have met their means.

Like Lincoln logs or Legos, being a true entrepreneur is ever changing and ever evolving while never giving up on your first mission statement. No matter how much we've grown, no matter how much we've learned, there is still that voice inside of us that tells us and drives us to be the best version of ourselves for ourselves and for our company/brand.

Remind yourself that the most successful companies started in a garage or basement or in the back of a car trunk. Some of the greatest inventions started by a note written on flimsy toilet paper or napkins. The only one getting in your way is you. You have the greatest shot to succeed. You have the greatest mind to make change. You have the greatest entrepreneur mind if you continue to put your passion into it. It's all about a healthy mindset. That's something I teach on a daily basis, because I choose to be that .2% of the world wanting to help others to improve their lives, to build a healthier mindset, to encourage self-growth, and believe in their personal life oasis to make the most out of their present day. As a matter of fact, I pride myself on helping others, writing their life stories by helping them to get rid of their anxiety, guilt, body shaming, depression, and even trauma to be their healthiest version of themselves.

My father was my biggest mentor and my greatest friend. He passed away when I was 11 years old, but his spirit and energy still humble me to this day. He told me when I was incredibly young, "If I did not learn something during my day, it was not a successful day." I believe it to be true that if you are loud enough to allow your success to make the noise, then you can surprise people almost daily. Walt Disney was famous for saying, "It's kind of fun to do the impossible." As entrepreneurs, we are always striving to do the impossible, to create something unlike anything we have seen, touched, or been in the presence of. We not only strive to make a living as a creative professional, but we strive to make a difference in our neighborhood, community, state, nation, and for some us, international recognition. Nonetheless, we all started from a seed planted somewhere. Some of us come from backgrounds as dishwashers, waiters, babysitters, or even house cleaners. For some of us, we have pushed the envelope every day against what our family expected us to be and continued to think outside the box to do the unexpected.

It is all possible with your customized key to success in fulfilling your network. Networking is a key. It is part of the secret sauce of branding. It is about who you know, what you know, and how your presence makes a difference. Your unique statement makes you stand out in whatever field you choose to pursue and is a staple to your present and your future. It is who you are when you shake hands. Your unique impact goes a long way. When someone meets me for the first time, it is uncommon for them to see me as an influencer above all else. Normally, what they see is a 30-year-old who is just getting started. I recognize I still have many challenges to overcome.

If I can change one person's life, to motivate, inspire and push someone to be comfortable with the best version of themselves, then all this hard-dedicated work has been worth it. It is now your turn to create your best life. You can start small or you can jump right in, just believe in yourself. Your big idea is the best idea, just leave room to evolve.

***

To contact Monica:

LinkedIn: https://www.linkedin.com/in/molovesolutions/

Facebook: https://www.facebook.com/molifeforyou/

Website: https://www.molifeforyou.com

Mike Skrypnek

BIG GOALS

"How can I give $1 million to charity every year, while building a sustainable business and great life?"

PROVEN SUCCESS

Mike is a transformational business coach, five-time author and international speaker. His Grow Get Give philosophy holds the keys to success that the world's most successful entrepreneurs know. He implemented it to achieve big impact in his life and the lives of thousands of entrepreneurs, business owners and the millionaire next door. His powerful message of giving back and growing business to achieve personal and professional success inspires others to set big impact goals for their lives.

IMPACT MINDSET

For his own big impact, he helped guide affluent families redirect $12.5 million in Big Impact Giving™, to charitable causes, and is committed to help entrepreneurs grow this to over $100 million.

GENEROUS WISDOM

With his proprietary, Mountain of Credibility™, training, Mike has trained hundreds of passionate entrepreneurs to learn how to gain top of mind positioning with their prospective customers in order to GROW their own unique business.

Mike can teach anyone how to manage their time and their talent better to GET more freedom to enjoy their lives and their family. His bestselling book, <u>Entrepreneur Secrets to a Grow Get Give Life</u>, is the perfect guide to show you how to GROW your business, GET more freedom and GIVE back.

How do you give $1 million to charity every year?

By Mike Skrypnek

A Shift from Hoarding to Giving

During the biggest global stock market crisis since the Great Depression, my life went through a major transition. Amidst the pressures of the 2008 market losses and stresses on my investment management business, I was battling with partners who had declining businesses and poor work habits who were selfishly enjoying the benefits of my intense work to keep our income coming in and assets growing.

A business divorce was the solution, but as in most break ups, only one party wants out, while the other holds on. So, despite being in the worst market decline in 80 years, I decided to move my business to another firm. Fear was at its pinnacle in the industry. Because of this, many of my clients were not willing to add moving to their concerns.

No matter how much I cared, or the successful track record of our past work, it felt like I was being blamed for the global market meltdown. I was painfully being measured for what I could not control.

I wanted more impact from my life. The economic crisis was the catalyst for me to break the pattern of "greed is good" and shift to "giving is good" by giving back during my day job, not just my evenings and weekends.

I wrote down this commitment on the whiteboard in my office:

"Give $1 million per year to charity"

I could give time, influence and even some money, but I didn't have $1 million "extra" to give away. So, the first step was learning how to build a business that supported my commitment to help charities and donors.

I started with The Strategic Coach™ program for guidance. Inspired with clear direction, I created a proprietary system, wrote research papers and within a year published my first book called *Philanthropy; An Inspired Process*.

My charitable prospects viewed me as the "fox-in-the-henhouse". They locked the barn, built fences and practically loaded their shotguns to keep me away. That first book was magical. It opened doors and served as a connection between my passion to give and my purpose to make a big impact through my investment business. By engaging a community of philanthropists, impact-minded entrepreneurs and giving families to guide them to the impact that they sought.

I knew nothing about giving a million dollars away to charity or building a business in my industry to sustain it. To serve the non-profit industry, I needed to learn, so I began to source coaches who had done it before.

My advisor peers were in the business of hoarding capital not giving it away. They called serving charity the "no-profit" industry. I was determined to prove them wrong. They dismissed my aspirations and didn't understand what I was doing. Caring and giving was not really the standard of the industry. It often seemed more like "make-and- take" and many of my coworkers' most important clients were themselves.

The market collapse and the unscrupulous behavior of former colleagues left my business beaten. Early on, I did not have industry partners or allies in my heart-centered drive to build a business on an impact-focused vision.

At the time my first book was published, my business had been decimated to a fifth of the size. My revenue had dropped to only 10% of two years prior! There was a ton of work yet to do to make a bigger impact in my life and the lives of others.

Fast-forward six years to 2016. I was gratefully an integral guide in nearly $12.5 million in charitable giving. My work had become nationally recognized and I was a dominant player in philanthropic estate planning. I published three more books on business and philanthropy and grew my revenues ten times bigger while diversifying my business into multiple unique revenue streams. All of which was value-added to my clients and my expertise.

Without hiring coaches to help direct me, I never could have figured it all out.

Working with great mentors was one of the most integral parts of my growth as a human being. Implementing their recommendations, transformed my business. From there I was seeking more freedom as an entrepreneur, more connection as a human and greater reach for impact. After helping baby boomers give and preserve their wealth to pass it on to future generations, I turned my attention to the business "builders" who were twenty years younger.

The financial industry felt confining with a soul-sucking daily routine. Working with entrepreneurs and business owners was exciting and limitless with conversations rich in hope and optimism. By sharing valuable wisdom gained through my accomplished baby boomer philanthropist clients, I could show entrepreneurs in real time how they could make their big impact.

My ten times business growth was built with a new passion to nearly $1 million in revenue and required a lot of work. I relied on great people and strong processes. Over $180,000 invested in a decade ensured I learned from some of the best coaches in North America. What made my business grow, how I was able to take more time off than ever before and make a huge impact could be taught to other entrepreneurs just like me when I started my journey.

With more freedom in my work, I could think and be creative. Aligning action with my passion, I envisioned helping one hundred impact-minded entrepreneurs earn more money while guiding each of them to redirect $1M from profits to charitable causes. Together, we could make a $100 million difference which seemed like an achievable goal. So, I set out to do just that.

Getting to My 'Why'

The goal to give more to charitable causes is my 'why' so I transitioned from legacy advisor to business coach. I left financial services to work with entrepreneurs and help them see the opportunities beyond themselves.

After a couple years focusing on building my new coaching business, things were going ok, but slow. On the surface, I had done all the right things: established credibility, developed a sound process, built a repeatable marketing system and a scalable model that attracted prospects to events. Large audiences would be able to drive even more business however, I ran into challenges attracting larger audiences when I moved cities. 'Frustrating' was a gentle way of stating my situation. There was something missing.

You see, my $100 million goal didn't explain much about why I could help or should be considered over other coaches. The big number didn't inspire or compel busy growth-focused business owners to want to start working with me. Then three conversations in thirty days happened.

Conversation one: I helped Launa write her book, *Getting Up*. She helped others get up and get back to business success after recovering from major life illness or trauma. We worked well together, enjoyed socializing and became great friends. She once told me, "You are intimidating, and people think you are a bit intense to approach." She then assured me, "Until they get to know you." Wow! I had never thought of myself that way. I suddenly became very aware of the perception people had of me and started smiling more. Seriously, smiling more!

Conversation two: I invested $97 for a one-hour conversation with Vaughn Pyne, who is a stellar guy, and new friend. He owns a corporate team training company. I wanted to get to know him better and possibly work with him on a project. During the session I asked him to walk me through his coaching process. He replied with one question: "Why do you coach?"

Vaughn is very intuitive. Probing, he asked me if it was so important to redirect more and more money to charitable causes, "Why don't you just stay in the financial services business? Why not serve entrepreneurs instead of baby boomers in that role?" I wanted to leave money management behind to be valued on the wisdom I had gained, to inspire the hearts and minds of motivated people. He asked again, "Why do you coach?" I had been contemplating this question already but didn't quite put my finger on it until then.

Over a two-decade career, there was no passion for me in the investment management profession I created. I learned from Nobel Laureates to be an expert in the science of investing and made prudent decisions for people in the management of risk and investment, but I never truly enjoyed it.

I thank Vaughn for unwittingly pressing me to share an important story that I have kept close to my heart for a long time. Let's review conversation three and I will share my story with you.

Conversation three: My amazing wife and business partner, Sherri, and I were driving home from a speaker's club event we hosted in Vancouver, BC. We were discussing the great evening and the stories that were shared. At the same time, I was disappointed with the low attendance compared to the high RSVP list.

This happened a couple times and my frustrations were coming out. I vented to Sherri. "Why the f*ck won't people show up? If they only knew how great the experience was, how much I can help them and how much I care, people would flock to these events." My clients knew this, and I wanted to help many more.

Sherri said, "You are a great speaker. Your stories are entertaining, and people love them, but you don't really get to the heart of things. You don't tell your real story."

She was right. Two decades in the financial service industry preserving a professional image and avoiding true vulnerability had prevented me from an honest explanation of my 'why'. From that moment, I would lay my intentions bare.

My "Real" Why

> *"Have you ever been fearful that you would be killed? Not that you might die from some known or discovered illness, not as a result of an accident, but fear that your life was endangered because you might be killed by someone you know, in a predetermined kind of way?"*

A couple years out of university, armed with a Kinesiology degree, and a rapidly growing personal fitness training agency business. I was a 23-year-old having a ton of fun with few concerns in the world. At the time, I was back living at my parents' place, working long hours and playing deep into the night.

My work life balance was nonexistent. The bad habits took their toll and I contracted mononucleosis. I was living life carelessly. Being sick highlighted how little I knew about running a business. I couldn't work and my business suffered. I felt like a captive while watching the entire OJ Simpson trial. This is when my path as a lifelong learner began. I discovered three amazing books, *Think and Grow* Rich by Napoleon Hill, *Seven Healthy Habits* by Stephen Covey and *Guerilla Marketing* by Jay Conrad Levinson.

Today, during my talks and workshops, that time is shared as a cautionary tale and one of enlightenment, illness and new focus for my life with attention to reading, business and marketing. But I'd never, ever talked about what was also going on at the exact same time until recently.

While living back at home in the basement of my parents' tiny home and for five evenings, in the middle of the darkest days of winter, before going to sleep, I'd lock the door to my bedroom worried that my father would come down the stairs and kill me in my sleep.

My dad has always been a thoughtful, caring and kind man and would never harm a soul. He also has schizophrenia which he endured since its unrelenting appearance in his late teens.

My parents' business was failing, the doctors were changing my dad's medication and he was in the darkness of deep depression. Things were bad and I imagined he might be contemplating suicide. My logic was that if he were to go through with it, he would think it better to kill me and my mother to save us the grief, and then take his own life. These were ominous times; I was worried and envisioned the worst outcome.

Keeping mental illness a secret was normal back then. At least within our family, when our parents shared the details of dad's illness, we were able to discuss it, demystify it and ask questions.

As part of my research for a first-year university psychology paper, I asked my dad about his experiences with electroconvulsive (shock) therapy. He loved Jack Nicholson and he described his early experiences diagnosed with schizophrenia as exactly like the movie "One Flew Over the Cuckoo's Nest", only with ten times more shock treatments. He believed had it not been for the ECT, he would not be sitting there telling me the story.

Having a manageable form of schizophrenia allowed him to function at a good level and we occasionally saw glimpses of his "Beautiful Mind" (without the paranoid delusions). We luckily had Jack Nicholson from the "One Flew Over..." institution and not Jack from "The Shining". For this I am eternally grateful. With medication, my dad was (and remains) a healthy, retired small business owner, loving parent and grandparent.

By all accounts, he is a mental health success story. But in that little window of time in 1994, what was going on for him (and my mother) would have been nearly unbearable for anyone. Balancing his brain chemistry was extraordinarily challenging.

Simultaneously, my parents were losing their business. Competition was growing and new bylaws increased costs for their portable sign company. In their tenth year of operations, they were working twice as hard for half the money. They owned a business, but it was really a job. They did not have freedom. During a Canadian winter, when it's -20 degrees Celsius and you're working outdoors, your business is going under, your house is at risk, and you're in your early fifties, crisis is inevitable.

For my dad, it was simply too much. He disappeared into his bed for weeks on end. My amazing mom was left to run the failing business, maintain the household, hold off the creditors and overcome challenges every single day. The body was on life support and she was making a valiant effort keeping the heart ticking. The entrepreneur dream they had worked so hard for in their lives was falling apart.

What lessons did I learn?

There were important lessons I learned because of my experiences, some realized then and others that I grew to learn over time.

The first of these lessons was that true entrepreneurial freedom comes when you own a business, not invest in a job. The ideal of entrepreneurship was there, but my parents worked so hard "in" their business that it burned them out. They were happy, but they weren't free and because their business could not function without them. They had no scale and could not make the adjustments necessary to react in deeply adverse conditions. When crisis arose, they almost lost everything. I would own my business, with no physical products, and either have others run it, or support it. It would be nimble and scalable and/or I'd be positioned to be compensated handsomely for my efforts.

The second lesson was to write books. Being and author is magical

The third lesson after a life of good and bad experiences is that there is no valor in the school of hard knocks. There is more value in good decisions, positive experiences and strong guidance. Experience is one thing, but avoidable tuition is another. While they provided a lot of great stories, a lot of my earlier years in business were a cautionary tale and demonstrated what not to do. School teaches you lessons and then gives you a test. Life gives you a test and you learn the lesson. That is wisdom.

The fourth lesson was simple. Hire high quality coaches and mentors.

The fifth lesson was learned after years of doing things the wrong way. My parents instilled strong independence in me. I never relied on others. Because of that, when I found mentors, they were often exciting people (with questionable ethics) and who used me but did not support me. My father was not able to be there, mentally, in my twenties as a mentor and my mother was too busy keeping the balls in the air. They cared deeply about me but did not have the capacity to help me objectively. My selection of mentors was terrible, and I repeated the pattern for nearly fifteen years. Like Luke Skywalker, I was lost, alone in the swamp, until I finally identified this repeating trait, stopped it then found great coaches and mentors. They changed my life now I dedicate myself to being the Yoda entrepreneurs need in their lives, committed to be there at that moment when I am needed the most.

Lastly, and most importantly, I learned that there are many things in life that are more important than work, money and fame. If you don't have your mental health or physical health, wealth success and accumulation will be worth nothing. I sacrificed a lot from time to time in my life journey, but health was never one of those things.

I hope sharing why I coach makes it clear as to exactly what people get when working with me. I care deeply and have wisdom to share generously.

Grow Get Give Coaching was created to reflect my philosophy of business and life. This guides me in teaching entrepreneurs how to GROW their unique businesses, wealth and impact; to help them GET more freedom to create, innovate and enjoy their life; and guide them to GIVE back to their family, community and the causes they care for most.

I have chosen to live my life in a way that allows me to check those boxes at all times.

***

Contact: info@mikeskrypnek.com

Website: www.GrowGetGive.com

Capture: www.growGetGiveSecrets.com

Phone: 604-898-46340

Linked In: https://www.linkedin.com/in/growgetgive/

Facebook: https://www.facebook.com/michael.skrypnek

Instagram: https://www.instagram.com/mikeskrypnek/

#growgetgive   #growgetgivesecrets

A Allen Hacker

A Allen Hacker is a self-help author, alternative psychology researcher, and personal and professional Self-actualization counselor. He has been a Master Journeyman carpenter, a successful custom home builder, and a casino manager.

As a business consultant he developed the Articulate Management business positioning system and the Affirmative Direction personnel management methods. As a counselor he developed Reticular Psychology and its Condition Assessment personal troubleshooting protocol, which uses advanced debriefing and strategic planning technologies to dissemble and replace errant thinking, from goals clarification to PTSD, in the context of a structured Self-actualization program.

Allen is a veteran and cancer survivor whose life's work is the relentless pursuit of the better understanding. He is the Founder of and Trustee for ASC Missions Group, ntc. ASC.org was established to create a whole-life set of missions to develop and deliver topically customized better understandings wherever possible.

A free online version of Allen's Effectiveness Profile self-improvement diagnostic program can be found at www.EffectivenessProfile.com For stress-driven outbursts, try his Stress Stabilizer at www.NetCoach.us

Subliminal Self Sabotage: Causes and Corrections

By A Allen Hacker

"Stinkin' thinkin.'" You may have heard this highly technical term. It's what Zig Ziglar calls the irrational thought patterns that unconsciously influence planning and decision-making.

Wendell Johnson (*People in Quandaries*, 1946) provides the most eloquent summary of how those patterns come to be: People tend to wrap themselves up into verbal cocoons, out from which they do not tend to hatch.

As a society accommodates increasingly varied knowledge, assumptions, and individual interests, it develops customs and rules to define common ground and minimize chaos. Customs and rules make it easier to negotiate differences within the bounds of acceptable behavior. But they also set and enforce those boundaries, too often creating rigid social boxes which can be equally as irrational as the average person's inner cocoons, and equally resistant to innovation.

The creative spirit suffers a tension within all that. One's own verbal cocoons inadvertently misdefine one's personhood and creative capacities and work to restrain one from full self-actualization. The social boxes tend to aggravate that problem by slanting general "permissions" toward the lowest common denominator, suppressing what comes to be known as creative disruption. Innovators must be willing to be a outliers whenever it becomes necessary to choose aspirations over acceptance.

Your mission, which you have accepted by embarking upon the self- and professional-development path is to come to terms with and step away from those cocoons and boxes.

How does subliminal self-sabotage come about? How does it work? How can you identify it? How can you free yourself from the stinkin' little boxes those cocoons become? To answer these questions and give you the best chance at success with the self-help exercise below, we must first touch on a bit of history and theory. You will see that our orientation is somewhat off the beaten path, but also that it has led to the resolution you seek.

The word, psychology, was invented over three thousand years ago by Greek philosophers and theorists. It was formulated as a title for the debate over the nature and location of the soul or spirit, or more literally, the "breath of life": What and where is it? The subject eventually divided into an argument between spiritualism and materialism, which then became a political football between the Church and the medical guilds. Each took turns at ownership until the Reformation, when the questions of spirit and consciousness were arbitrarily divided. The Church kept the spirit and exorcisms, and doctors took the brain and surgery. Which, in a way, left the excluded middle open for independent examination. A wide spectrum of people began to explore the lost essence of psychology itself: consciousness.

That is where we come in, looking into the officially excluded middle where few study or even speak of the psyche, and yet acknowledge that the materialists' results are dismal. We find that the better results come from addressing the individual as that which is conscious rather than as a biochemical phenomenon. We discuss the details of that elsewhere. Here, we focus on answering the above questions from the perspective that consciousness is an attribute of the psyche and that "the mind" is not an object but rather an activity comprising a set of functions such as perception, contemplation, thought, meditation, and information processing, all of which we call mentation.

Mentation is most constructively viewed as a holistic aggregation of all of the above and more, including the response mechanism that manifests as emotion. We include the emotive mechanism because it can be verbally articulated and analyzed.

Mentation is a corruptible process. Misdefinition, erroneous information, contextual confusion and emotional distortion are the most common factors.

Emotions are felt resonance and dissonance with respect to the degree of consistency between the current state of affairs and the individual's objectives and standards. "Positive", or desirable emotions, flow from gratification while "negative", or resisted emotions, flow from the objectionable.

We resist having our standards violated, the more strongly so as those standards are precious to us. For example, we dislike having our honor besmirched, but we absolutely abhor having our bodies maimed or our lives terminated. Our response is to resist such events. Conversely, we enjoy having our standards met or gratified, and the more so, the more we like it. We enjoy being respected, but we love to be loved. Yet each desire includes a dark space for resistance an absence of fulfilment. Resistance to the absence of a desired thing can invert to become demand for it, which then can lead to impulsive and even addictive behaviors. The more valued the standard, and the more egregious its violation, the more intense the associated emotion will be when a violation occurs.

Most misdefinition happens during traumatic or unhappy emotional experiences.

We all go through life defining things for ourselves, and sometimes getting things wrong. We can misdefine ourselves, and we can misdefine other people and the world itself. Bad assumptions made under duress—and invisibly inserted into the thoughts we have about everything.

Alfred Korzybski (*Science and Sanity, 1933*) told us that the map is not the territory. A map is never a perfect replication of reality. Therefore, trying to follow an old map can make for a rough journey.

General Semanticists call this "semantic error": false meanings, correlations and/or interpretations. Too often, semantic error is the road to disaster.

In Computer Land, the entire problem is summed up as GIGO. Garbage In, Garbage out. Give a computer bad information or programming, and if it doesn't just freeze up, it will give you garbage back. Ditto mental garbage.

There is a non-traumatic emotionally neutral form of misdefinition, which is simply incorrect information. It's different because of its lack of associated intensity and so requires its own category because it can't be reliably identified by peering into the usual feelings. Although it is the cleanest (and therefore most invisible) form of semantic error, it does cause enough confusion to require mention.

Next, we must consider the nature of memory.

Think of memory as a formless volume of holographic mist. Every place and event you have ever experienced, every thought and imagining you have ever had, every person you have known and more, all are represented there, in full-motion sensory realism. All it takes to replay any of it is to put attention on it. Purposefully or incidentally, it makes no difference.

Everything in the mind is very elaborately (and often improbably) cross-referenced. Attention can flow through the most intricate and often illogical connections imaginable to wind up in some wildly surprising places. This often renders some very strange conclusions compared to what is actually going on. All faster than thought itself, and too often unnoticed.

Mentation is an imaginative process independent of space and time. It is multidimensional, potentially employing infinite intermeshed holograms simultaneously. Multiple scenarios are compared simultaneously, each including its own time, location and effect projections. At its pinnacle, mentation is parallel processing squared—everything all the time. Because all of the parts of a complex process can occur simultaneously, the result of a thought often occurs at the moment it begins. This is where our hopes for human potential lies. Our difficulty, too.

Context sensitivity is the correlation and connection of events, objects and information by similarities and significant differences. This is discernment. It's how we know what is and isn't relevant to the topic or scenario at hand, and in magical moments, it is how we make inspired connections toward invention. The difficulty appears when resistance makes any of one's analysis or decisional elements invisible.

"Betty" was knocked down in the doorway of a bakery by a skateboarder she hadn't seen coming. Dizzied, and shocked by the pain, she had fallen sprawled onto the floor like a neglected rag doll. She recovered physically, but her life did not. She had become afraid to leave her apartment, and her was losing her close relationship with her father, a retired baker himself.

"Paul" bought a used car with most of his money right out of school. After a month of escalating breakdowns and expenses that left him in debt with a car that still gave him trouble, and the salesman never calling him back, he seriously suspected that the salesman had intentionally defrauded him. When he went to seek reimbursement, the much older and aggressive offender laughed in his face and dared him to "Just try me!" Paul folded up inside and just walked away. Years later, and despite having had a successful management career, when he started his own company, he couldn't get past his unexamined hatred to invest in his own sales department.

These events violate several of Betty's and Paul's standards for how things should be. They resist every one of those violations and in so doing reframe their standards toward the negative.

Betty should not hurt; she should not lie about in an undignified position; nasty surprises should not happen; one should be able to walk out a door safely; she should be able to handle it; life is supposed to be fun; the world is supposed to be friendly; and, People should be careful!

Paul should not be cheated, people should be honest and not liars and thieves, and never trust a used car salesman! Or any salesman, because they're all just after your money in the end.

Each of these violations becomes a mental object of resistance, elements they wish to avoid hidden in the cracks within memories they are not willing to re-experience. Henceforth, each will strive to prevent such things from happening, but in their avoidance not think why. They gradually change toward pessimism without really noticing.

Betty and Paul suffered trauma and reacted badly, formulating perspectives that didn't work later. Betty's trauma was physical, and Paul's was emotional, but that's where the difference ends. The reaction and subsequent loss of self happens the same way for each of them.

What is truly different, however, is the simple information error.

"Bill" had become known for a gambling problem that had caused him horrific embarrassments throughout his years living and working in Las Vegas. None of the usual societies and therapies had worked for him. Then one day, quite by accident, a set of innocent circumstances caused his attention fo jump back to an event as a child when a cousin had given him a bad definition: A casino is a place you go to get money. Well!

Bill saw that his understanding of casinos was a fallacy except when you work in the casino and the money you get is wages and tips. His entire perspective on casino gaming shattered and restructured in an instant. By the time he finished laughing at the silliness of his error, his gambling problem had vaporized.

Semantic error, then, is one or more operative but skewed mentation factors that you don't notice while you are looking at everything else. Or actually that you won't see because you are unwittingly avoiding looking at the memories within which they live.

When your knowledge and experience are all neatly correlated and catalogued, you have a rational knowledge base you can easily refer to and build from. But what do you have when major portions of your reference base are rendered invisible by resistance and exaggerated by misplaced emotion?

We call that kind of entanglement reticulation. A thing is said to be reticular if its structure is characterized by a web of cross-linked pathways. There are two anatomical examples in the nerve bundles that connect the eyes to the brain: the retina within each eye, and the reticular formation deep in the visual cortex where the two bundles intricately intertwine and then explode out into the brain.

If you are a rock hound, you've probably seen the geological version, reticulated quartz. This is when transparent quartz stone is beautifully "contaminated" by filigree of metals such as copper or silver that became trapped along the crystalline structures within the quartz as it cooled into solid rock.

From this word we've derived a special name for those gobs of mental and emotional spaghetti we so fondly know as, 'Stinkin' Thinkin'. We call one of those a reticulum. And from that, through more than twenty years of research and application in a business consulting service geared toward blockbusting mental barriers to success, we have developed what we refer to as reticular psychology: a non-linear object-oriented method of describing irrational mentation and a specially-structured technology for dismantling and reorganizing it. That process is at the core of the self-help exercise that follows.

There are a few things you should know before you explore and use our exercise. First, because reticulation is non-linear and object-oriented, we have found that there is no need to spend a lot of time and discomfort finding and reliving old events and emotions. The narrative is just an envelope; the message is inside. So, this exercise doesn't try to reduce the trigger reaction in a traumatic incident. (For a different exercise that does that in acute situations, see the link below.)

The exercise presented here is a short form self-help version derived from our primary block-busting technology, the Condition Assessment. It simply plucks out individual elements from the reticulum upon which the unwanted condition lives, until the reticulum itself crumbles. At that point, the combination of elements that formed the foundation and mechanisms of the subliminal sabotage ceases to exist, deleting the manifest problem.

Second, in formal session this all happens within a structured Q & A using a well-established universe of data types that targets and draws forth the client's objects of resistance and exposes them to conscious inspection, automatically terminating them. This works because it is not possible to resist and inspect a thing at the same time. A successful "look" instantly converts the items from resisted and hidden to accepted and properly correlated.

Third, Step three asks you to apply the phenomenon of cognitive dissonance. Therefore, you must understand cognitive dissonance. Based on the root words for mismatched sounds (and thus meaning not resonant), cognitive dissonance is the discomfort (dizziness, disorientation, etc.) that occurs when a person tries to hold two or more conflicting ideas in mind at the same time.

Incompatible ideas won't synch up, so trying to fit them together puts you into a discomfiting mental loop of switching back and forth between or among them. You can find yourself simultaneously going toward and bouncing away from each. You never really master either or any of them, and instead find yourself experiencing a strange sensation of being suspended in a vibratory back-and-forth kind of nowhere.

That's why cognitive dissonance is uncomfortable, unpleasant, and even a strange kind of painful. It's a signal that something is amiss.

Yet it is perfectly safe to access. Any physical symptoms are only mind-over-matter effects from the body getting caught up in your mental activity. Just stay relaxed and take it easy. Of course, you should be sitting somewhere quiet as you do this.

Because cognitive dissonance can be so noticeable, you can use it as an accessibility signpost to your as-yet unnoticed conflicted mentation. You will experience the dissonance as you approach the offending items before you even see them. The trick is to willingly experience it with an openness to its content.

Fourth, you must suspend all judgement while doing this. Don't concern yourself that most of what you get is nonsense–that's why it's a problem! But don't skip over the perfectly logical either, because nothing always works exactly the same way in every situation.

And Fifth, Take it easy. The view will improve as you progress through the exercise.

The exercise follows. It shouldn't be expected to be as effective as the formally delivered process, but it certainly can remove a significant amount of cloudiness and frustration from your pursuits.

1. Begin with the obvious clue: something is repeatedly going wrong, in much the same way every time. Work out a first-impression general statement of what that is. Not why, but what and how, as far as you can tell.

2. Ask yourself, "What keeps happening that I don't want?" Write it down and give it a descriptive title or name. Repeat until you have a clear statement of the problem.

3. While watching for any sign of cognitive dissonance and looking at your written statement of the problem, ask yourself, What's behind that? Write down everything that comes up. You can also ask for alternative forms of that question, such as, What's in that? Write down everything that comes to mind, repeating the question and writing answers until you've asked it at least three times with nothing new coming up.

4. Create a separate column for each side of the dissonance and/or all of the conflicting thoughts. (There may be more than two "sides"

to it.) Rewrite each of the items you listed in Step 3 into the most appropriate column.

5. Write a description of the world and future implied by each column.

6. For each world and future, write a description of the self you would have to be to live there.

7. Choose your desired world from among them, or if none of them catch your fire, abandon them all to look for an even better idea that describes a more desirable world by your own standards. You can use opposites and "insteads" to develop the items you'll want in your world, your future, and the self you want to be.

8. Write out an affirmative description of what your preferred world looks like. Not what it's not, but what it is when it becomes real. Include yourself in that description, and make it entirely affirmative with no negative verbiage, no use of any form of the word No, or Not. That will both keep you on track and serve as a platform for noticing any further subliminal time-bombs.

9. Notice and add to your notes any arguments that bubble up against any of your desired points.

10. Cycle back through the exercise until you have what you want at Step 8. Then,

11. Adopt that new thinking, become that self, and live into that world.

BTW, stress is the cognitive dissonance of desperately wanting to be somewhere (or anywhere) else. There's a quick Stress Relief exercise you can use to de-escalate "triggered" (stress-activated) unwanted behavior. You will find it in the links below.

***

To contact Allen:

Email: Speaker@ASC.Org or A@AllenHacker.com

Websites, www.ASC.org and www.AllenHacker.com.

A free online version of his Effectiveness Profile self-improvement diagnostic program can be found at www.EffectivenessProfile.com

Danielle Edmondson

Danielle is the Founder, CEO of Angelosophy. A devoted believer in Christ, mother of two, Lifestyle Medicine Coach and Certified Yoga Teacher. She is also the Owner/CEO of StemLIGHT Holistic Wellness, Regenerative Therapy in Center in Texas. And supports women in her private coaching practice, teaches children's yoga camps and offers holistic wellness workshops and retreats.

Danielle has 20 years' experience in coaching and inspiring women in self-healing, self-discovery and realigning with their life purpose. She is passionate about supporting children in their God-given nature. And is currently working toward opening a spiritual and holistic wellness center called the LIGHT Ranch for families that will offer the LIGHT School, a holistic enrichment program for children.

Danielle is an American patriot and committed to the global collaboration toward spiritual sovereignty and unity consciousness and fully aligned with the global mission to end human/sex trafficking and slavery.

She is passionate about supporting women and children on their life path and wholeheartedly believes in the essence of humanity. Her purpose in life is to reveal light in the world by embodying love and sharing the Angelosophy mission as an "Ambassador of LIGHT" for the expansion of light on earth and beyond.

Angelosophy: Ambassador of Light

By Danielle Edmondson

I would like to begin by saying thank you Jim Britt for reaching out to me to be included as a co-author of this book. It is an honor and true manifestation in God's timing to share Angelosophy through this entrepreneurial platform. May God bless you, Kevin, Tony and all who are connected to this endeavor to share and spread more light globally!

Angelosophy is a mission to support the holistic and spiritual wellbeing of women, children and family with a servant purpose of revealing and expanding light on the earth for healing and harmony of our planet. Essentially, Angelosophy represents the action of "being the light" in the world.

Hello, my name is Danielle Edmondson and I AM an "Ambassador of Light." Being a devoted spiritual teacher and lover of the light is my inspiration to inspire the world to connect to our Creator, the "unified quantum field" source of all creation, to heal, prosper and thrive!

As a human being you have a unique gift that is a part of your soul's blueprint to serve humanity in a specific way and is an important part of our collective consciousness destiny. Your internal LIGHT plays a crucial role in the destiny of God's plan. YOU are an important part of the divine matrix design and the wellbeing of humanity thriving as whole! You can make a difference in the world! How exciting! I believe we are spiritually called to action to serve. And when we commit to this action our lives can prosper abundantly in every aspect of our life. By design.

It begins with being accountable for the choices we make in our life. I believe true FREEDOM is ACCOUNTABILITY for oneself. When we take personal responsibility for our thoughts, emotions, actions and more importantly our RE-actions in our life, we become empowered in our lives. Identifying and letting go of any victimization mentality is instrumental to the process. This is the first line of defense toward overcoming the challenges in our life and stepping into a life of more freedom and joy. Living by example as an expression of love and light to those around you while being the brightest light we can be for the highest good of mankind is the action. Sounds like a lot of work and responsibility doesn't it? It is and it's not. It's a personal choice and the essential role of our journey to overcoming the limitations that distracts us from embodying this action on a daily basis. It takes commitment, passion and discipline. I trust a person will come to the realization that it is the most spiritually sovereign choice you can make that will support you in choosing true happiness and joy in your life. Yes, happiness is a choice and has a vibrational frequency. The key is to resonate with it.

No one can make you feel unhappy. That is an illusion and victim reality. Sometimes you may choose to react to a person that triggered your emotional state. It is up to you to choose the vibration of happiness no matter who or what the situation may be. Don't give your joy away. And if you do find yourself in an unhappy vibrational frequency, stop and be present with yourself. Ask the universe in that moment why, what, where and how? Why do I feel this way right now? What was the trigger for me to shift into this energy? Where did this state of being originate from my past experience? How can I shift back into a state of happiness right now? Then listen with awareness for the answers. They might come in a form of thoughts, feelings, and visions or sometimes later through someone else's actions that are a mirror to yours. The answer will present itself by continuing to ask until the universe shows you through what you attract in your life. This may take time. It takes time to strengthen this practice and receive results. The more you practice this exercise it becomes second nature and when you ask these internal questions the answers will eventually come instantly and then you have the power to shift it in that moment authentically. Once you have awareness of this subconscious limitation you can bring the LIGHT to it for healing. This will raise your frequency and that emotional trigger will no longer be limiting you from slipping into a lower frequency. You will be more conscious of it and next time have the opportunity to choose to stay in the higher vibrational state regardless of your environment. It truly is a life changing healing modality. Try it and see how it works for you!

What blocks a person from choosing this higher state of being? Subconscious programming. No matter where you came from, your past does not have to define who you are in the present moment in a negative way or "lower frequency." As human beings living our day to day lives this comes with overcoming challenges. No matter how small or overwhelming humanity still finds a way to overcome adversity and move forward in life. The good news is we can do this in a faster more efficient way through shifting our personal vibrational frequency rather than taking years to sit in therapy sessions and talk about past painful memories that will only strengthen the current neuropathway programs in our brain. Practicing these meditative exercises every day by connecting to the light within will support shifting the energy and create new higher vibrational programs that will change our experience and environment around us.

You have the power to change your subconscious imprinting and programming by transforming your energy to a higher vibration through self-awareness and spiritual consciousness. The more we raise our personal vibrational frequency of light through daily spiritual practice and caring for our body holistically we move into balance and harmony in our lives. I call this Lifestyle Medicine for the Soul. And I love teaching and coaching people in living their life in optimal, "high vibrational" wellbeing.

Caring for our LIGHT Body plays a role in our vibrational frequency. What we consume also holds a vibrational frequency. The food we eat, the air we breathe, the water we drink, our thoughts and feelings as well as the people and environment around us all have an effect on our quantum field. It is our choice to be mindful of these energies we choose to consume or let consume us on a daily basis. They can support us in expanding and maintaining our energy in a positive way or these energies can participate in keeping us ill in a lower frequency. Illness can only exist when our DNA's light voltage is low. Therefore, we have the power, no pun intended, to heal dis-ease through raising our frequency within. Hence, letting go of the powerless victim energy and embodying our true divine light nature through self-love and care of our body, mind and spirit.

Being stewards of our LIGHT vessel in this world is more than an action, it is a responsibility of service to the universe. As I shared before we are all light beings on the earth, connected through the unseen quantum field of consciousness. Our subconscious and conscious choices have an effect on each other as well as it does on the universal light that is expanding every day. We are here on this earth plane to heal our ego state and move into the 5th dimension of consciousness where peace and harmony exist. I always tell people you can do this the easy way or the hard way. Why not consciously commit and join forces to being an Ambassador of LIGHT on earth for the sake of humanity thriving again? Or for the interest of your children's future and your own spiritual sovereignty? I promise you it is more fun and much more rewarding in life to be your highest vibrational self. It takes interpersonal work yes. And it takes less energy than living your life in chaos looping in a suffering state of being. You have the power to change yourself in any moment. By design. So, I say choose your light path and change the world!

Very different from children, we as adults have to deprogram and reprogram our subconscious minds. Essentially, we have to rewrite our personal life script. It is our movie and we are the Director, Producer and the Star. So, what does your life movie project out into the world? It's yours to co-create with God and yours to share in the world. So, I say make it a masterpiece because whether you realize it or not you are the masterpiece God made you to be. Claim it! It is written. Ephesians 2:20- For we are God's masterpiece. He has created us anew in Christ Jesus, so we can do the good things he planned for us long ago.

Embody love in all you do and cherish the life you have been given. Most of all share your light and serve others around you. Your light will shine, and you will essentially "represent the light" to those around you as Jesus taught us through his example. What a gift this is and when you do this the light on the earth and beyond expands. It brings healing and harmony to realities we may not be aware of yet are connected to through the quantum field of light. We truly are unified, and it is our duty to be aware of what we are putting out to the universe in our expression of self. Every choice has an effect on the light body of the whole. Whether we are conscious or not. So, I say be conscious of your subconscious thoughts and be in control of your feelings. What you put out is what you get back. It's an energetic ripple effect. I have always loved the verse and do my best to live by it, "Do to others whatever you would like them to do to you. This is the essence of all that is taught in the law and the prophets." Matthew 7:12

When we do this, we are "Being the light" on earth and beyond. Mathew 5: 14-16 "You are the light of the world. A town built on a hill cannot be hidden. [15] Neither do people light a lamp and put it under a bowl. Instead they put it on its stand, and it gives light to everyone in the house. [16] In the same way, let your light shine before others, that they may see your good deeds and glorify your Father in heaven."

If we did this, I believe the world would be in a sacred space in a higher dimension than third dimensional reality (3D). We would shift into the 5D state of consciousness. This is the intention of the new paradigm today. Raising our frequency so we shift our consciousness into the fifth dimensional reality where wars, poverty, and hunger do not exist. Only prosperity consciousness and love. How do we support this becoming a reality as the collective? By understanding that we are all one in the light of God. That separation is an illusion. The door to this consciousness is being accountable for our individual nature and doing the work to upgrade our life condition by raising our light body's vibrational frequency to embody love. Which most importantly becomes a powerful mirror to our children.

Our children learn from what we do and say and most importantly it is what we show them with our actions in the choices we make for ourselves that they become imprinted by. The key is "walking our walk" AND "talking our talk" at the same time with integrity, love and authenticity. That is why being accountable for our inner state of being reflects how we project our light in the world. And our children experience this and even more importantly mimic what we do, say and feel. Conscious or subconscious they mirror our reflection. So, it is very important to be our best selves and do our interpersonal and spiritual light work so we can be our highest expression for our children and ultimately humanity's wellbeing. How awesome is this that we have this amazing gift of free will to resurrect ourselves in any moment we choose? We as individuals have the power to change our lives and the world!

Which leads me to sharing my love for supporting and nurturing children in their divine nature so they can be the light they came to be from the beginning of their life on earth. They are already in the highest frequency of love when they come into the world. It is our duty to the light to preserve the innocence of our children and their unique light in this world. Why is it so important to create a sacred space for the children of today to be who they came into the world to be? It is their birthright from God and children are the future of our society. We should honor these light beings. Just because they are little humans doesn't make them less important until they are adults. I believe they are the most important. We should be supporting them in ways that will help them preserve the purity of their light from the day they are born. Imagine if you were supported in this way from early development. Where would you be today? Who would you be in the world today?

It is time we create a new way of supporting children by focusing on teaching them practices of staying connected to source energy every day by supporting them in strengthening their intuitive and spiritual gifts. And getting back to the basics of life through creativity, nature, family values and the Christ light within. This will support humanity in thriving into the future. Children essentially have always been the future. It took many generations to get to the reality of our world today. I realized the education system was inferior when I was girl growing up. Children are bored in school today and I hear some say how the hate to go to school. I don't like hearing the statement from adults "well no kid really likes to go to school." Do you hear the problem in that statement? Kids should love to learn and want to learn and be excited about it. I believe if you teach a child the skill of learning, they are set for life. They can learn anything their heart desires. How? Because they are connected to God who has all the answers they seek. And will guide them on the journey of learning to be exactly where they are supposed to be in alignment with their blueprint. This is why teaching a child to meditate changes the world. Teaching a child how to grow food and how plants work in the body to support wellbeing changes the world. Teaching children that accountability is freedom and joy. Teaching children to love the light of God, themselves, and those around them changes the world.

Imagine a beautiful ranch where children can create, learn, play, grow and expand their inner light just by being the expression they choose to be in the world. Doing yoga, meditating, riding horses, and gardening, making art, dancing, playing music and being in nature on a daily basis. A place for the whole family to connect. This is what I call the LIGHT Ranch. It is a sacred space for families to come and practice being the light in the world. A place to get back to the basics of life, leave the cell phone at the door and reconnect to who they truly are by being present in the moment with themselves, their children and those around them. Lifestyle medicine for the whole family! I am working toward creating that space and until then I will continue to teach ways to expand our light on the earth and serve humanity in the ways God guides me to.

What does being in service to others mean to you? How would you define service in your life? As entrepreneurs we love to create and innovate! The question is what is our motivation and inspirational intention for what we do every day? Is it to serve our clients and customers, or humanity as whole? Are we embodying the servant spirit authentically? Are you being the light in the world on a daily basis? What areas of your life could you raise your frequency in that would serve you and those around you? These are all questions that are empowering in one's life and if everyone asked these questions and took responsibility for their spiritual sovereignty, we would find ourselves in a world of peace and harmony.

In the face of our society living in uncertain times I continue to believe in the heart of humanity and I am certain the light will prevail on the earth in spite of the dark negative forces we battle each day. God gave us free will and this amazing gift called life that we get to co-create with the source of all creation. We are protected and supported by this unified field of consciousness and the more we believe and take the time to connect to the unseen realm the more we will expand our light, attract abundant prosperity and live in peace and harmony forever. The quantum unified field exists for the purpose to love and support us in transforming our lives into the expression of our hearts desire.

Every human being has been given the opportunity to crack the rich code by choosing to resonate with the highest vibrational frequency of love and prosperity consciousness in their life. It is up to you in this moment to choose to be the light in the world in all you do.

May God bless you on your life journey in all aspects of your destiny to embody spiritual sovereignty on this earth and beyond...

In loving memory of my Mother Eleanor Lorraine Edmondson 1943-2020

***

To contact Danielle:

Danielle Edmondson

512-800-0816

http://www.angelosophy.com/

https://www.stemlightcenter.com/

Facebook:

https://www.facebook.com/Danielle.angelosophy/

https://www.facebook.com/angelosophy/

https://www.facebook.com/thelightranch

https://www.facebook.com/lightschoolkids

https://www.facebook.com/HideaBible

https://www.facebook.com/healforhumanity.us

YouTube Channel: Angelosophy

https://www.youtube.com/channel/UCKl-bZlpACku6ERdikYr4sA?view_as=subscriber

Afterword

Life and business are always a series of transitions... people, places, and things that shape who we are as individuals. Often, you never know that the next catalyst for improving your business and life is around the corner, in the next person you meet or the next book you read.

Jim Britt and Kevin Harrington have spent decades influencing individuals and entrepreneurs with strategies to grow their business, developing the right mindset and mental toughness to thrive in today's business environment and to live a better life.

Allow all you have read in this book to create a new you, to reinvent yourself and your business model if required, because every business and life level requires a different you. It is your journey to craft.

Cracking the Rich Code is a series that offers much more than a book. It is a community of like-minded influencers from around the world. A global movement. Each chapter is like opening a surprise gift, that just may contain the one idea that changes everything for you. Watch for future releases and add them to your collection. If you know of anyone who would like to be considered as a co-author for a future volume, have them email our offices at support@jimbritt.com

The individual and combined works of Jim Britt and Kevin Harrington have filled seminar rooms to maximum capacity and created a worldwide demand. If you get the opportunity to attend one of their live events, jump at the chance. You'll be glad you did.

If you are a coach, speaker, consultant of entrepreneur and would like to get the details about becoming a coauthor in the next Cracking the Rich Code book in the series, contact Jim Britt at support@jimbritt.com.

To Schedule Jim Britt or Kevin Harrington as a featured speaker at your next convention or special event, email: support@jimbritt.com

Master your moment as they become hours that become days.

Make it a great life!

Your legacy awaits.

STAY IN TOUCH

www.JimBritt.com

www.JimBrittCoaching.com

www.KevinHarrington.tv

For daily strategies and insights from top coaches, speakers and entrepreneurs, join us at:

THE RICH CODE CLUB---FREE members site.

www.TheRichCodeClub.com

www.ingramcontent.com/pod-product-compliance
Lightning Source LLC
Chambersburg PA
CBHW071351290426
44108CB00014B/1498